Dare
to
Hope

*The prophet Jeremiah thought he had
legitimate reasons for carrying negative
thoughts when he wrote the book of
Lamentations, but suddenly he realized he was
engaged in a battle for control of his mind. He
could rehearse the negatives or he could begin
to hope. He could dare to hope! Then his
darkness turned to light—the light of hope. He
seemed amazed at himself when he said:*

"Yet I still dare to hope!"

Wellington Boone

Dare
to
Hope

A 30-Day
Journey to Hope

"Yet I still dare to hope."
(Lamentations 3:21)

Dare to Hope
A 30-Day Journey to Hope
My Journey with God Series #2

© 2009 Wellington Boone

www.daretohopejournal.com
www.apptepublishing.com
www.wellingtonboone.com

Library of Congress Control Number: 2009908507
ISBN: 978-0-9776892-8-6

Printed in the United States of America
February 2010

PUBLISHED BY APPTE PUBLISHING
5875 Peachtree Industrial Blvd. Suite 300
Norcross, GA 30092

770-840-0888

My Personal Dare to Hope Journal

I began my 30-day Countdown to Hope in The Year of our Lord

(Starting date and year)

(Sign your name)

"Yet I still dare to hope."
Lamentations 3:21

CONTENTS

INTRODUCTION

SECTION 1. GETTING THE MOST OUT OF YOUR JOURNAL

Chapter 1.	Preparing to Meet Your Maker	7
Chapter 2.	Using Your Journal to Develop Your Inner Strength	11
Chapter 3.	Developing a Christ-Like Holiness Standard	15
Chapter 4.	Sharing Your Holiness and Hope with Others	17
Chapter 5.	Getting Blessed by the Bible	19
Chapter 6.	Living the Sacrificial Life	23
Chapter 7.	Praying for Israel	25
Chapter 8.	Walking in Prosperity	27
Chapter 9.	Understanding Your Journal	29
Chapter 10.	Be a Finisher!	31

SECTION 2. YOUR PERSONAL DARE TO HOPE JOURNAL

Including a Great Story of Enduring Hope in Each Day's Journal

2A. THE TRUE MEANING OF HOPE

Day 1.	Hoping that God Accepts You *(Fanny Crosby)*	36
Day 2.	Hopeful Because God Values You *(William Booth)*	42
Day 3.	God's High Hopes for You *(Jonathan Edwards)*	48
Day 4.	God's Hope That You Will Be Like Jesus *(Hiram Revels)*	54

2B. BECOMING A HOPEFUL PERSON YOURSELF

Day 5.	Cultivating God's Presence to Release Hope *(George Fox)*	60
Day 6.	Building Hope From a Place of Humility *(Harriet Tubman)*	66
Day 7.	Commanding Your Soul to Hope *(Robert Smalls)*	72
Day 8.	Releasing Hope by Forgiveness *(Corrie ten Boom)*	78
Day 9.	Restoring Hope by Repentance *(James McGready)*	84
Day 10.	Increasing the Reach of Your Prayers by Hope *(John Knox)*	90
Day 11.	Hope for Financial Independence *(Maggie Walker)*	96

2C. HELPING OTHERS BY YOUR HOPE

Day 12.	Deciding to Have Hope for Others *(John Wesley)*	102
Day 13.	Uniting Families Through Hope *(Frederick Douglass)*	108
Day 14.	Sacrificing in Hopes of Others' Change *(Charles Finney)*	114
Day 15.	Hoping Your Donations Make a Difference *(Lewis Tappan)*	120
Day 16.	Sanctifying Yourself to Spread Hope *(Thomas Johnson)*	126
Day 17.	Hoping for a Harvest of Souls *(Charles Spurgeon)*	132
Day 18.	Changing Society by Hope *(William Wilberforce)*	138
Day 19.	Replenishing Hope of the Poor *(George Washington Carver)*	144
Day 20.	Praying for Hopeless Sinners *(Father Daniel Nash)*	150
Day 21.	Preaching Hope from a Warehouse *(William Seymour)*	156
Day 22.	Inspiring Hope by Writing *(Harriet Beecher Stowe)*	162
Day 23.	Sustaining Hope Under Fire *(John Calvin)*	168
Day 24.	Hoping to Be the Light of the World *(Francis Asbury)*	174

2D. HOPE AS AN ETERNAL QUALITY

Day 25.	Eternal Value of Hope *(David Brainerd)*	180
Day 26.	The Next Dimension of Hope *(Horatio Spafford)*	186
Day 27.	Ever-Increasing Hope *(D.L. Moody)*	192
Day 28.	The Splendor of Hope *(The Puritans)*	198
Day 29.	Hope of Eternal Life *(Catherine Booth)*	204
Day 30.	Hope of a Kingdom under Christ *(Toccoa Falls Flood)*	210
Conclusion.	Where Will You Go from Here?	216

SECTION 3. THROUGH-THE-BIBLE READING GUIDE

KEY EVENTS AND ANSWERS TO PRAYER THAT BUILT YOUR HOPE

INTRODUCTION

Jeremiah lamented, "He has filled me with bitterness.
He has given me a cup of deep sorrow to drink.
He has made me grind my teeth on gravel.
He has rolled me in the dust. Peace has been stripped away,
and I have forgotten what prosperity is."
Then he exclaimed—

"Yet I still dare to hope."

(Lamentations 3:15-18, 21).

Do you still have the courage to hope? If you listen to the news very
long today you can easily lose hope. News anchors don't know what
else to do with all the bad reports they receive so they unload them on you.
When you listen to all that negative news, it stays in your mind unless you
make one important decision: *You must dare to hope!* Decide to remain
hopeful regardless of the news, the people around you, or your own
personal crises. Dare to hope!

Hope is enduring. It comes from God. It gives you vision so you
can flourish in the midst of apparent failure. It gives you the strength to
overcome negatives. It is a character quality of Christ-likeness that can be
developed through diligence. This 30-day journal is a journey to hope.

The love chapter is also a hope chapter

First Corinthians 13 is called the "love chapter" of the Bible. However, it is
also a hope chapter. It equates a hopeful attitude with coming of age and
Christian growth.

"When I was a child, I spoke and thought and reasoned
as a child does. But when I grew up, I put away childish
things. Now we see things imperfectly as in a poor
mirror, but then we will see everything with perfect
clarity. All that I know now is partial and incomplete, but
then I will know everything completely,
just as God knows me now.
There are three things that will endure—
faith, hope, and love"
(1 Corinthians 13:11-13).

Hope is an enduring quality, but if you are not vigilant you can allow yourself to lose hope. Anyone can focus on the negatives. It takes a mature person to focus on hope and positive outcomes, but it's worth it. In 30 days, this journal will help train you to look at life from a position of hope. It will develop qualities of Christ-like hope that will make you strong and help you to create an environment of hope for yourself and those around you.

The prophet Habakkuk rejoiced in the God of hope Who was greater than his negative circumstances. He said even though everything seemed to be going wrong, "yet I will rejoice in the LORD!"

> *"Even though the fig trees have no blossoms, and there are no grapes on the vine; even though the olive crop fails, and the fields lie empty and barren; even though the flocks die in the fields, and the cattle barns are empty, yet I will rejoice in the LORD! I will be joyful in the God of my salvation"*
> *(Habakkuk 3:17-18).*

Forget the negatives and be hopeful!

All of us make daily choices. We decide to be happy and full of hope or we decide to be sad and full of despair. We make up our minds whether the stuff going on around us will get us down or we will rise above it and take on hope. Negative minds dwell on disturbing news stories and sad personal experiences and bad things that have happened to them or to others they know. If you aren't careful, negative thoughts can dominate your thought-life. That's why you need hope. Hope defeats death and despair and releases you from the pain of the past into a new life of joy and power.

Forget the past!
Philippians 3: 13-14 KJV

"But this one thing I do, forgetting those things which are behind, and reaching forth unto those things which are before, I press toward the mark for the prize of the high calling of God in Christ Jesus."

When you carry painful thoughts day after day, your pain follows you into your future. It is not because the wound hasn't been healed or the situation hasn't been resolved, but because you choose to keep the wound open through your thought-life.

When you choose to carry hope with you instead of despair, hope rescues you from the negatives and takes you into a future full of light. Old wounds are healed and forgotten. You discover that you still dare to hope!

God values how you spend your time because He values you!

God puts a value on how you spend your days. Why? Because He puts a value on you! How you spend your life is important to Him!

As you follow the journal's instructions for daily accountability, your hope will increase. You will see what you did with your time so that you can make changes and be ready to present yourself before God to receive His "well done." You will be blessed by God as you seek to understand what He wants to change in your life, then make those changes.

As you use this journal to examine your life daily, your journal will bring to light everything that drains your hope so you can get rid of any habits of darkness and never be without hope another day in your life. These practical and spiritual exercises will increase your intimacy with God because you will develop Christ-likeness as you build your hope.

BUILDING YOUR HOPE DAY-BY-DAY

Dare to Hope is a system of 24-hour personal accountability—a foundational set of daily disciplines that will give you a new passion for knowing God and a new pleasure in pleasing Him.

In the back of the book you will find a guide for reading through the Bible. Each day you will read Scriptures and a devotional page teaching you how to build hope by spending time with God and His Word.

You will read inspiring vignettes of Christians like these who dared to hope they could overcome adversity and change their generation:

- Harriet Tubman, who believed she could not only escape from slavery but also rescue others—300 by the time she was done
- John Calvin and John Knox, who overcame persecution to reform the Church and build systems of government based on the Bible
- Charles Spurgeon, an English preacher who drew crowds to his church from the time he was just 19 years old in spite of ill health
- William Wilberforce, first elected in his 20s, who fought against entrenched powers to end slavery in the British empire
- John Wesley, mocked for his college "Holy Club" and barred from preaching in churches but bringing an international spiritual awakening and founding the Methodist Church

Those are a few of the 30 stories about Christians whose radical commitment to Christ and daily disciplines of hope, faith, and love allowed them to boldly change their world.

How your journal builds intimacy with God and hope

Every day as you read your journal and complete the exercises you will increase your hope level and you will also:

- Become more sensitive to the Holy Spirit.
- Overcome negative thinking.
- Read and meditate on the Word and be inspired to write.
- Be excited by historical vignettes of successful people.
- Set fruitful prayer priorities for your time with God.
- Become accountable to God for your time and money.
- Do reasonable service toward God and man.
- Never go to sleep without a clear conscience.
- Increase your passion to transform yourself, your family, church, community, nation, and the world as God speaks.

WHY JEREMIAH DARED TO HOPE

Jeremiah thought he had legitimate reasons for carrying negative thoughts when he wrote the book of Lamentations, but suddenly he realized he was engaged in a battle for his mind. He could rehearse the negatives or he could begin to hope. He could dare to hope! Then his darkness turned to light—the light of hope. He seemed amazed as he said:

"Yet I still dare to hope" (Lamentations 3:21).

It doesn't matter what is going on in your life or what terrible news you have heard lately. You can turn off your pain just like you can turn off negative TV news. Turn off sadness and turn on hope! Take your pain to God. He can restore you to health and the spiritual prosperity that comes through hope. Your present may not look too promising at the moment, but your hope can change your future.

Section 1

Getting the Most Out of Your Journal

CHAPTER 1

PREPARING TO MEET YOUR MAKER

" 'God sets himself against the proud,
but he shows favor to the humble.'
"So humble yourselves before God.
Resist the Devil, and he will flee from you.
Draw close to God, and God will draw close to you"
(James 4:4-8).

You may have heard the old saying "Prepare to meet your Maker." When you meet with God in daily devotions, you are meeting with your Maker. The starting place in meeting God is joy that your heavenly Father wants to spend time with you, but you have to keep the right context. You need to remember His greatness and power.

Humbling yourself to find true intimacy with God

God is greater than you are. He is greater than your understanding and therefore you need to humble yourself and place your trust in Him. Submit to Him and acknowledge and obey what He tells you in your time alone.

Private, intimate time with God is a sweet privilege that comes about through yieldedness. It is rewarded by grace and power.

David wrote, "My meditation of him shall be sweet: I will be glad in the LORD" (Psalm 104:34 KJV). He knew God loved him and he loved being with God.

Making *God's needs* your first priority, not *your needs*

As you set aside time to pray, read the Bible, and write in your journal, you will be making God your focus instead of anything else. You read the Bible not out of duty so that you can say, "I was in the Word today." You read for fresh revelation from God. You enter into His divine rest.

"For he that is entered into his rest, he also hath
ceased from his own works, as God did from his"
(Hebrews 4:10 KJV).

You are spending time with Him to find out about *His* needs and *His* priorities for your life. You are saying by your lifestyle that you don't need anything else more than His reality. As much as you love your spouse, your children, your parents, or your friends, you love God more.

Taking time to develop intimacy

When you are alone with God, don't let anything else get in the way. If I have to, I will drive to a parking lot to get away from everyone and everything that would distract me from God. Sometimes I still have to walk away from the ministry to be alone with God and to fast and pray. I stay for forty days in isolation.

Through time alone with God, you develop intimacy. You cultivate your friendship with the Holy Spirit, Who is very sensitive. He works first with every Christian alone and He's easily grieved when He is not given private attention. God is jealous over anything that we choose to do instead of spending time with Him.

Becoming still to become like Christ

For most of us, our lifestyles are an enemy to quietness, but the Scripture says, "Be still and know that I am God" (Psalm 46:10 KJV). The word "know" is the same word used for sexual intimacy. You need intimacy with God more than you need television, entertainment, or even time with family and friends. He wants to be your total focus.

God, your greatest Friend, is calling you to be alone with Him. Do you know the sweetness of prayer? Do you love spending secret time with God alone? Will you lay aside every weight to become like Him?

"Wherefore seeing we also are compassed about with so
great a cloud of witnesses, let us lay aside every weight,
and the sin which doth so easily beset us, and
let us run with patience the race that is set before us,
Looking unto Jesus the author and finisher of our faith;
who for the joy that was set before him endured the
cross, despising the shame, and is set down at the
right hand of the throne of God"
(Hebrews 12:1-2 KJV).

Turning over your schedule to God

Give God your schedule. Most of us are driven by the demands of our time when we decide what we should do with our day. However, your human mind is too limited to understand God and His will. You can't put God on any kind of rational time scale and try to figure him out logically. You have to know Him on the inside through yielding and spending intimate time with Him in the closet of total surrender before you will understand His plans and timetable for your daily life.

Using accountability to come into Christ-like hope

God's goal for you is Christ-likeness. The ultimate goal of this personal accountability *Dare to Hope* journal is shaping you into His image so you can say with sincerity, "I represent Jesus."

> *"For whom he did foreknow, he also did predestinate to*
> *be conformed to the image of his Son, that he might be*
> *the firstborn among many brethren"*
> *(Romans 8:29 KJV).*

God can use your journal to make you more aware of how a godly lifestyle increases your level of hope. Your lifestyle can become such an example of righteousness that people will know a man or woman of God is among them and they will turn to you for hope.

BEGINNING AND ENDING YOUR DAY WITH GOD

Sometimes people ask me if it makes any difference whether they pray and read the Bible in the morning or if they can wait until the evening before they go to bed. Yes, I believe it does make a difference.

Beginning your day with God

Jesus arose a great while before day. So did many of the saints of old. Don't try to enter the day without first spending time in the morning to give your day to God. Whatever you do in the evening is only a completion of that time in the morning.

Seek Me early to find Me Proverbs 8:17 KJV	*"I love them that love me; and those that seek me early shall find me."*
Jesus arose a great while before day Mark 1:35 KJV	*"And in the morning, rising up **a great while before day**, [Jesus] went out, and departed into **a solitary place**, and there prayed."*
God wakens me every morning Isaiah 50:4 KJV	*"[H]e wakeneth **morning by morning**, he wakeneth mine ear to hear as the learned."*

Ending the day with final accountability

John and Charles Wesley with their 18th-century Holy Club at Oxford prayed privately and wrote down their prayers during the day. Each night, they reviewed the affairs of the day, repented as necessary, and made new resolutions. Before they went to sleep, they recommitted themselves to the care and protection of God. As a result, they slept in peace. At the end of your day, finish anything incomplete in your quest for Christ-likeness.

QUESTIONS TO ASK YOURSELF AT THE CLOSE OF EACH DAY

- Did I give praise and thanksgiving to God for something today?
- Do I need to repent for anything?
- Did I stay humble enough in the midst of challenges?
- Have I neglected my reading, in the Bible or otherwise?
- Do I still need to pray for anyone?
- Did my schedule today reflect a commitment to do the will of God?
- Did I leave undone any acts of kindness that I should have done?
- Are my financial affairs in order?
- Am I preparing for future financial and spiritual prosperity?
- Do I need to take a walk or otherwise complete my exercise?
- Have I controlled my time today, or has it controlled me?
- Did I spend my time doing anything that offended God?
- Did I sleep too much? Eat too much? Watch too much TV?
- If I died tonight, would the Lord say to me, "Well done"?

- *May I go to sleep now, Father?*

CHAPTER 2

USING YOUR JOURNAL TO DEVELOP YOUR INNER STRENGTH

"Trust in the LORD with all thine heart; and
lean not unto thine own understanding.
In all thy ways acknowledge him, and
he shall direct thy paths" (Proverbs 3:5-6 KJV).

A s you proceed through this journal with humility and hope, the Scriptures will come alive to you. Your prayer life will increase in depth and sensitivity. You will be inspired by the lives of people of the past and see that you can become a godly person like them. You will grow in your ability to make right choices that lead to Christ-likeness.

Personal accountability by great Christians of the past

Many of the Christians of the past whom we consider great today examined their lives daily to expose where they were unlike Christ. They recognized that daily practices of accountability prepared them for that Great Day when God would ask them to give a final accounting of their lives before the Judgment Seat of Christ. They would be ready to hear Him say "Well done" because they had sought His approval every day.

Many of them recorded the events of their daily lives in journals and held themselves accountable in writing each day in two areas:

1. How they spent their time in godly pursuits

2. What they did with their money

Judging yourself so you will not be judged

By keeping a journal of how you spend your time in godly pursuits and what you did with your money, you can judge yourself daily and develop the inner strength that comes from being righteous. You will learn how to please God like Christians of the past and, more importantly, as Jesus pleased His Father. Pleasing God will become your most important goal every day. You will be willing to sacrifice sleep, food, and fellowship with others just for the privilege of being with Him. You will discern the level of your spirituality. You won't have to live with guilt, because you are ordained to be free. You will dare to hope!

JOURNALING YOUR INSIGHTS (REVELATIONS)

A revolution begins with the spoken word, but it is carried by the pen. This journal provides places where you can document in writing what you learn and what you hear from God that could bring a spiritual revolution to you and your generation. Personal revelations that come as you pray and seek His face are worth writing down for yourself and others.

You may think that God already has enough men and women teaching His Word, but somebody, somewhere, needs to know what *you* hear in the atmosphere of consecration and total surrender.

*"Write down what you have seen—both the
things that are now happening and the
things that will happen later" (Revelation 1:19).*

As you read and study the Bible and become inspired by the lives of the great Christians you read about every day, write down insights that come as you become more sensitive to His will and purpose for your life.

WHAT TO WRITE ABOUT IN YOUR JOURNAL

- Your increasing depth of understanding of Who God is
- Your journey into Christ-likeness
- Your insight into the Scriptures
- Your increased patience and perseverance in times of trial
- Your impressions of the Christians whose lives you read about
- Your passion to go after the lost
- Your good works and what God will say about them
- The truth you learn about yourself in personal accountability
- Your ever-increasing hope

Developing inner boundaries through accountability

Daily accountability helps you to become more orderly and to grow in spiritual maturity. We start with *outer* boundaries from the time we are children, but adults need to develop *inner* boundaries. *Dare to Hope* provides outward boundaries of documentation that point you toward the development of inward boundaries of Christ-likeness. Inner boundaries come from the Creator. Those are the ones that God is after ultimately.

> *"But he is a Jew, which is one inwardly;*
> *and circumcision is that of the heart, in the spirit,*
> *and not in the letter" (Romans 2:29 KJV).*

Letting your journal locate you

As you work through your journal for the next 30 days, you will build hope that you can accomplish God's will in earth, as it is in heaven—both the entire earth, which is the world around you, but even more important, in *your* earth, which is the ground of your heart.

God's focus will be your heart. That is the area that needs to be changed first. God will help you, through Jesus Christ, with the Holy Ghost as your Guide, to develop a changed heart.

Search	*"Search me, O God, and know my heart: try me, and*
my heart	*know my thoughts: And see if there be any wicked*
Psalm 139:23-24 KJV	*way in me, and lead me in the way everlasting."*

This journal will show you where you are on the map of your personal walk with God and then give you directions about where to go next so that you can lay the foundation for a godly, hope-filled life. All day long you will keep account of yourself before God. At the end of each day, after you complete your journal, you will be able to judge for yourself where you are, just as God will be able to judge you at the end of your days on earth. You will know what you have thought, read, and done all day that you now have to offer to God at night.

I WANT A PRINCIPLE WITHIN
By Charles Wesley
(1707-1788)

"I want a principle within of watchful, godly fear,
A sensibility of sin, a pain to feel it near.
I want the first approach to feel of pride or wrong desire,
To catch the wandering of my will, and quench the kindling fire.

"From Thee that I no more may stray, no more Thy goodness grieve,
Grant me the filial awe, I pray, the tender conscience give.
Quick as the apple of an eye, O God, my conscience make;
Awake my soul when sin is nigh, and keep it still awake.

"Almighty God of truth and love, to me Thy power impart;
The mountain from my soul remove, the hardness from my heart.
O may the least omission pain my reawakened soul,
And drive me to that blood again, which makes the wounded whole."

CHAPTER 3

DEVELOPING A CHRIST-LIKE HOLINESS STANDARD

*"I am crucified with Christ: nevertheless I live; yet not I,
but Christ liveth in me: and the life which I now live in the flesh
I live by the faith of the Son of God, who loved me, and
gave himself for me" (Galatians 2:20 KJV).*

God wants you to look like Jesus, but Jesus didn't leave a picture of Himself so you could compare yourself with how He looks physically. The photograph that God wants you to show that represents who He is has your face painted on it. You are like Jesus to the degree that you surrender.

When you are like Jesus—

You please the Father. The desire to please Him is your driving motivation.

You are holy. You have power over sin, both in yourself and others. You become a dynamic force.

Holiness purifies your heart, which leads to reconciliation among families, races, denominations, and socio-economic levels.

Holiness transforms and unifies churches and releases the fruit of the Spirit to be active among Christians.

Revivals and spiritual awakenings are birthed when Christians enter an intense search for personal holiness and God hears them and gives them the power to save sinners.

Unbelievers respond to a Christian whose heart's desire is to be holy. They become born again and begin to clean up their lives, with a resulting transformation of society.

HOLY PEOPLE OF GOD

Jesus	*"And the angel answered and said unto her, The Holy Ghost shall come upon thee, and the power of the Highest shall overshadow thee: therefore also **that holy thing** which shall be born of thee shall be called the Son of God" (Luke 1:35 KJV).*
John The Baptist	***"For Herod feared John, knowing that he was a just man and an holy, and observed him**; and when he heard him, he did many things, and heard him gladly" (Mark 6:20 KJV).*
Prophets	*"As he spake by the mouth of his **holy prophets**, which have been since the world began: That we should be saved from our enemies, and from the hand of all that hate us" (Luke 1:70-71 KJV).*
Barnabas	*"For he was a good man, and **full of the Holy Ghost** and of faith" (Acts 11:24 KJV).*
You	*"I beseech **you** therefore, brethren, by the mercies of God, that ye present your bodies a living sacrifice, **holy**, acceptable unto God, which is your reasonable service" (Romans 12:1 KJV).*

God calls you to be holy, like Christ. If that were not possible, He would not have given you that standard. ***You can be holy.***

CHAPTER 4

SHARING YOUR HOLINESS AND
HOPE WITH OTHERS

"Our Father which art in heaven, Hallowed be thy name.
Thy kingdom come. Thy will be done in earth,
as it is in heaven" (Matthew 6:9-10 KJV).

As a pastor, I recognize that my dedication is not only for me. It is also for those who rely on me to minister to them every week. My personal devotion to God can make the earth more like heaven for all.

As the Church—the Body of Christ—we can prepare to transform society by developing holiness and hope in ourselves.

My prayer is, Lord, make me so yielded now that
I will not have to cry over my failures when I get to heaven.
Provoke me now to come up another level in
holiness and total consecration.
Help me to sow seeds of destiny into others' hearts
so that they desire above all else to
know You and to become like Your Son, Jesus Christ,
in every thought, word, and deed.

Heavenly minded people help others experience heaven

The whole matter of eternal realities is understated. Jesus prayed, "Thy will be done in earth as it is in heaven" (Matthew 6:10 KJV). When you are heavenly minded, that is when you can do the most good in the earth.

In America, Christians were the first colonial governors. They built the first universities and hospitals. They had the vision to fight for freedom from tyranny and oppression. Through faith they were able to survive slavery—if they were Black—or defeat it if they were White.

Until you see heaven's reality in the secret place with God, you won't understand the urgency of bringing heaven to earth in the way that Jesus prayed.

If you want to feel good about yourself, you need to make God feel good about you. You want Him to be encouraged that you are doing your part to make earth like heaven because you represent Jesus.

God has only one standard, and it is based on His holiness. Sin gives you a temporary illusion of power, but it's not true value. Nothing around you is like heaven when you are in sin.

When you're secure in Him, you bring His standards into every relationship. People can count on you just as they can count on God because you are trying to represent Him in every thought, word, and deed.

God loves you with an unselfish, sacrificial love and He wants you to love others in the same way, too.

CHAPTER 5

GETTING BLESSED BY THE BIBLE

Jesus said, "My mother and my brethren are these
which hear the word of God, and do it" (Luke 8:21 KJV).

E ach day as you read the Bible and listen to God alone, prayer and
Scripture will become the anchors of your day. Like the Bereans of
Acts 17, you will become known as "noble" as God blesses you by your
reading of the Bible and fills you with understanding of the Word.

Reading four chapters of the Bible daily

When I speak in the churches of many different denominations, one
question always receives the same response. I ask, "How many of you read
your Bible every day?" Fewer than 50 people ever raise their hands, even if
the audience is in the thousands.

When I ask those same people, "How many of you eat food every
day?" All of them raise their hands. Which food will last you for eternity,
physical food or spiritual food? Most people don't consider that what they
are eating from the Word of God today is preparing them for tomorrow and
also for eternity. They don't eat the Word of God as if their life depended
upon it and as if the realm it represents is real.

Authority of the Scriptures, which are true and fully accurate

At the time of the Protestant Reformation, one of the stands taken by
Martin Luther, John Calvin, John Knox, and other Reformers was "*Sola
Scriptura*"—Scripture Alone! To receive the greatest benefit from the
Bible, acknowledge that it is inerrant—the true and accurate and literal
Word of God. Martin Luther took a public stand for salvation by grace
alone—not by works dictated by man—that he never heard about in church
but read about in Romans. All of the Reformers constantly reaffirmed the
truth of the Scriptures beyond the interpretation of any man, even though it
might mean persecution or even death.

JESUS AND THESE GREAT MEN SAID THE BIBLE IS TRUE

Jesus said that "the scripture cannot be broken" (John 10:35 KJV). The Scriptures would be fulfilled as long as heaven and earth remained (Matthew 5:18, 24:35; Luke 16:17). His life fulfilled Scripture (Matthew 26:56, Luke 24:27, Luke 24:44-46).

Luke said that understanding of the Scriptures comes from Jesus (Luke 24:45).

John said that Jesus' life fulfilled Scripture (John 19:28; 19:36-37).

Paul said, "All Scripture is inspired by God and is useful to teach us what is true and to make us realize what is wrong in our lives. It straightens us out and teaches us to do what is right. It is God's way of preparing us in every way, fully equipped for every good thing God wants us to do" (2 Timothy 3:16-17).

Peter said, "Above all, you must understand that no prophecy in Scripture ever came from the prophets themselves or because they wanted to prophesy. It was the Holy Spirit who moved the prophets to speak from God" (2 Peter 1:20-21).

Martin Luther said, "The great unthankfulness, contempt of God's Word, and willfulness of the world, make me fear that the divine light will soon cease to shine on man, for God's Word has ever had its certain course."

John Calvin said, "Scripture indeed is self-authenticating; hence, it is not right to subject it to proof and reasoning."

Josephus wrote in his secular history written independently of the New Testament the same details of history we find in the Bible.

The Dead Sea Scrolls include Old Testament passages like Isaiah 53 that confirm that prophecies of what would happen in Jesus' life were written before His birth.

The Original Constitution of the Colony of New Haven (June 4, 1639) said that "the scriptures do hold forth a perfect rule for the direction and government of all men in all duties which they are to perform to GOD and men, as well as in families and commonwealth."

When you read the Bible as truth, you can see the end from the beginning. You can see that God has ordained a hopeful end for you and all of creation. You believe God for those things which are not seen as though they are already seen. You become like Abraham, who "against hope believed in hope" (Romans 4:18 KJV), when the angel told him as an old man that he and his aged wife Sarah would have a son.

America's only hope for true liberty

America's founders acknowledged the truth of the Bible and incorporated the Word of God into their laws and colonial covenants. In spite of Supreme Court rulings to the contrary, America is blessed because it is built on the Bible, Jesus Christ, and the Church.

On the Liberty Bell in Philadelphia is an inscription from Leviticus 25:10 that proclaims the year of Jubilee, the Lord's Release:

"Proclaim liberty throughout all the land."

Only God can release a nation into true liberty. America's only hope—and your only hope—is found in the Word of God. Those truths are an everlasting foundation for all that is good. When Christians with a heart for America know the truth and speak the truth in love, people will listen and find hope.

THROUGH-THE-BIBLE IN ONE YEAR READING GUIDE

The Through-the-Bible Reading Guide in the back of this book is a daily reading list of four chapters from eight different sections of the Bible. Not everyone will start this guide on January 1. When you begin your journal, just find that day's date and start reading there. In that way, all of us will be reading the same four chapters of the Bible together on the same days of the year.

The Bible contains 1,189 chapters (Old Testament,
929 chapters; New Testament, 260 chapters).
Reading 4 chapters per day, and repeating Proverbs and
the End Times books of Daniel and Revelation, you can
read every chapter in the entire Bible in 12 months.

Eight divisions of the Bible used in the reading guide:

Pentateuch. Genesis, Exodus, Leviticus, Numbers, Deuteronomy

History. Joshua, Judges, Ruth, 1 Samuel, 2 Samuel, 1 Kings, 2 Kings, Ezra, Nehemiah, Esther *(1 and 2 Chronicles are read at the end of the Epistles. Acts is read after the Gospels.)*

Poetry. Job, Psalms, Song of Solomon *(Ecclesiastes is read at the end of the Prophets.)*

Wisdom. Proverbs *(repeated during the year)*

Prophets. Jeremiah, Lamentations, Ezekiel, Hosea, Joel, Amos, Obadiah, Jonah, Micah, Nahum, Habakkuk, Zephaniah, Haggai, Zechariah, Malachi *(Isaiah is read after the Gospels and Acts.)*

Gospels. Matthew, Mark, Luke, John *(followed by Acts and Isaiah)*

Epistles. Romans, 1 Corinthians, 2 Corinthians, Galatians, Ephesians, Philippians, Colossians, 1 Thessalonians, 2 Thessalonians, 1 Timothy, 2 Timothy, Titus, Philemon, Hebrews, James, 1 Peter, 2 Peter, 1 John, 2 John, 3 John, Jude *(followed by 1 and 2 Chronicles)*

End Times. Daniel, Revelation *(repeated during the year)*

CHAPTER 6

LIVING THE SACRIFICIAL LIFE

"Gather my saints together unto me; those that have made a covenant with me by sacrifice" (Psalm 50:5 KJV).

Y ou may not yet know your specific calling and you may not have all of the education you need, but your dedication can help you to accomplish God's will. This journal will help you build your dedication.

"And so, dear brothers and sisters, I plead with you to give your bodies to God. Let them be a living and holy sacrifice—the kind he will accept. When you think of what he has done for you, is this too much to ask? Don't copy the behavior and customs of this world, but let God transform you into a new person by changing the way you think. Then you will know what God wants you to do, and you will know how good and pleasing and perfect his will really is" (Romans 12:1-2).

Sacrifice of fasting

During these 30 days, set aside times for fasting, even if it is only an occasional meal or other sacrifice related to food where you deny yourself. Try to increase as you go along.

Fasting helps you to experience a deeper relationship with God. It is an example of the death-life principle—dying to self for the sake of the kingdom. You don't give your lusts any rights. You forbid your body to have preeminence.

Isaiah 58 speaks of the fast that brings light, healing, protection, and answered prayer:

"If you do these things, your salvation will come like the dawn. Yes, your healing will come quickly. Your godliness will lead you forward, and the glory of the LORD will protect you from behind. Then when you call, the LORD will answer. 'Yes, I am here,' he will quickly reply" (Isaiah 58:8-9).

When you make a commitment not to eat, whether it is one meal, one day, or one week or 30 or 40 days, and you make it through, you gain a satisfying sense of accomplishment in addition to any results you see from your prayers. Especially when you go on an extended fast you become full of faith for what God can do for you supernaturally.

Jesus said, *"When you fast"* (Matthew 6:16) not *"if you fast"* because He expected His disciples to fast. He fasted for 40 days, and we know that the number 40 represents testing.

Fasting breaks through your inner turmoil and clarifies what you believe and what you should do. The devil likes to mess with your mind and he hates to see Christians fasting because fasting breaks every yoke.

Fasting is God's age old prescription for breaking bondages. It is not optional for Christians. The work of deliverance that Jesus has called us to do is too important to neglect this spiritual discipline that will empower us. God is calling us to fast and we must obey.

Fasting takes you above your circumstances and your needs into the realm of eternity where God is.

Sacrifice of serving

"Your attitude should be the same that Christ Jesus had.
Though he was God, he did not demand and cling to his
rights as God. He made himself nothing; he took the
humble position of a slave and appeared in human form.
And in human form he obediently humbled himself even
further by dying a criminal's death on a cross.
Because of this, God raised him up to the heights of
heaven and gave him a name that is above every other
name, so that at the name of Jesus every knee will bow,
in heaven and on earth and under the earth, and
every tongue will confess that Jesus Christ is Lord, to the
glory of God the Father" (Philippians 2:5-11).

Christians are destined to be godly rulers like Christ—both in this world, and the next (Revelation 22:5). However, before God can trust you with authority, He will take you through a training program in humility.

When you are humble, God can give you power because you won't use it for yourself. You will be a servant leader, not a self-serving leader nobody can touch. You will be like Jesus.

CHAPTER 7

PRAYING FOR ISRAEL

"O children of Abraham, God's servant,
O descendants of Jacob, God's chosen one.
He is the LORD our God.
His rule is seen throughout the land.
He always stands by his covenant—
the commitment he made to a thousand generations.
This is the covenant he made with Abraham
and the oath he swore to Isaac.
He confirmed it to Jacob as a decree,
to the people of Israel as a never-ending treaty" (Psalm 105:6-10).

Israel is unique among the nations of the earth.

God promised to give Canaan to the Jews, even when the land was already occupied. The world may reject Israel's claim to its land, but God stands by His Word forever. He still chose Israel as His people. The Jews reject Jesus as their Messiah, but the Bible says that they will ultimately recognize their wrong and receive Him. As we see Israel searching desperately for answers, we must pray diligently to that end.

"Then I will pour out a spirit of grace and prayer on the
family of David and on all the people of Jerusalem. They
will look on me whom they have pierced and mourn for
him as for an only son. They will grieve bitterly for him
as for a firstborn son who has died" (Zechariah 12:10).

Israel represents God's elect. When you bless Israel, you will be blessed, but when you curse Israel, you incur God's wrath.

"I will bless you and make you famous, and I will make
you a blessing to others. I will bless those who bless you
and curse those who curse you. All the families of the
earth will be blessed through you" (Genesis 12:2-3).

Prayers for Israel:

- Pray that Israel will know the true and living God,
- Pray that the people will acknowledge Jesus as their Messiah
- Pray that America will remain a friend of Israel, even if all the rest of the world treats Israel as an enemy.
- Pray for the peace of Jerusalem.

"Pray for the peace of Jerusalem.
May all who love this city prosper.
O Jerusalem, may there be peace within your walls
and prosperity in your palaces.
For the sake of my family and friends, I will say,
'Peace be with you.'
For the sake of the house of the LORD our God,
I will seek what is best for you, O Jerusalem"
(Psalm 122:6-9).

CHAPTER 8

WALKING IN PROSPERITY

". . . the LORD thy God: for it is he that giveth thee power to get wealth, that he may establish his covenant" (Deuteronomy 8:18 KJV).

God wants you to prosper—not only spiritually but also economically. In your journal under "Money Management and Wealth" you will be able to develop your financial portfolio in prayer and consecration. Piety does not have to mean poverty.

God owns all the wealth in the world, but most of those who control it are sinners. God wants *Christians* to steward His wealth, not sinners. If you don't have much money to manage for God, maybe you haven't gone after it seriously enough. Maybe you have believed there was something sinful about having money.

When you are rich, doors open to you. You can become a person of influence. You can be a producer instead of a consumer. You can provide finances for the people of God so that they can be about the Father's business without becoming distracted by raising money. You can meet not only your own needs but also the needs of your family, church, and those in need. You can leave a godly inheritance—natural as well as spiritual. You can be like the patriarchs of the Bible.

If you are rich in prayer, rich in the Word of God, rich in consecration, why should there be anything wrong with also being rich in money? Somebody is handling the resources of the world. Why not you? You can be a bank instead of going to a bank. You can be a lender whom others come to, not a borrower begging for a loan. You can be empowering businesses instead of looking for others to empower you. If your pastor wants a new building, you can be the first in line with a check. You just have to keep your heart right.

"Cry out for insight and understanding. Search for them as you would for lost money or hidden treasure. Then you will understand what it means to fear the LORD, and you will gain knowledge of God. For the LORD grants wisdom! From his mouth come knowledge and understanding" (Proverbs 2:3-6).

If the love of money does not dominate your life but the love of God's wisdom and the fear of the Lord, you can be trusted with handling money—both yours and someone else's. Even if you don't yet manage money well or if you haven't learned to see managing money as a demonstration of the orderliness of God, you can change! Make that one of your goals during the next 30 days.

CHAPTER 9

UNDERSTANDING
YOUR JOURNAL

Each day in your *Dare to Hope* journal you will find spiritual and practical exercises that will build your hope as you increase your intimacy with God through personal accountability.

The *opening Scripture* sets the theme for the day and lays a solid foundation on the Word of God.

The *daily devotional on hope* explains how your hope level increases as you build your relationship with God and follow His Word.

In the chart for your *Through-the-Bible Daily Readings* you will look in the back of the book to find the readings for that date, then write them in. If you have any thoughts on those passages as you read, you can write them down in your journal.

In *My Prayer Priorities for Today* you will find a list of categories for prayer beginning with the most important—your right relationship with God. Sometimes in setting prayer priorities Christians have used as a guide Paul's advice in 1 Timothy 2 to pray first for "kings and all who are in authority," but God's first priority in your prayers is *you*. How well are you listening? Are you following Him and becoming like Christ? From that foundation you can pray for all of these concerns:

- *My right relationship with God*
- *Needs of family and friends*
- *Fivefold ministry church leadership*
- *Leaders—local, state, nation, world*
- *Worldwide revivals and awakenings*
- *Praise and thanksgiving*

Following the prayer priorities you will find a *quote from a famous Christian* whose testimony is included in that day's reading.

Under *Money Management and Wealth* you will find a place where you can make notes about managing your present finances and also develop ideas for future financial prosperity.

This is followed by a *Scripture that declares the good future that God has for you.*

In *My Treasure Chest of Hope* you will be able to increase your hope level by writing down what God has done for you in the past as well as your dreams for the future.

- *Counting My Many Blessings*
- *Planning My Hopes and Dreams*

Each day you will read one of the *Great Testimonies of Hope* describing how some Christian of the past dared to hope and pressed through obstacles to fulfill God's will. You will be able to write notes about how these testimonies affected you and what they inspired you to do.

In your *24-Hour Personal Accountability Journal* you will document your day so that you can look back and see how dedicated you are by how you spent your time. You can see yourself as God sees you.

Today's Journal of Personal Insights gives you a place to write down what God is showing you from the Scriptures, prayer, and life!

A *Scripture on self judgment* reminds you of how much God values your willingness to judge yourself and evaluate how you live.

In *My Self-Evaluation—How Well Did I Do Today?* you rate the categories of personal accountability as you record what you have done, experienced and learned, and what God has done for you.

- *Family time*
- *Praise, worship and thanksgiving*
- *Prayer and extraordinary prayer*
- *Time with friends*
- *Reading and meditating on the Word of God*
- *Reaching the lost*
- *Fasting and other sacrifices*
- *Eating right and exercising*
- *Serving others in Christ-like love*
- *Organizing myself to serve God*

The day concludes with a *Scripture on hope* and a reminder of the *Days Remaining in Your Countdown to Hope.* The countdown theme comes from Lamentations 3:21 (counting down 3-2-1), *"Yet I still dare to hope."* At the end of the countdown, you will have a habit of hope.

CHAPTER 10

BE A FINISHER!

". . . let us lay aside every weight, and the
sin which doth so easily beset us, and let us
run with patience the race that is set before us,
looking unto Jesus the author and finisher of our faith"
(Hebrews 12:1-2 KJV).

As you begin your journal, make a commitment to finish in 30 straight days. In sports, do pros quit before the final buzzer? Of course not. Athletes play to the finish and they play to win! Christians should never have a quitters' mentality. Jesus wasn't like that, and neither are you.

Jesus came to finish *John 4:34 KJV*	*"My meat is to do the will of him that sent me, **and to finish his work.**"*

Jesus in you becomes the champion of finishing for you. He pioneered finishing. With Christ in you, you can finish anything that begins in God's purpose for your life.

To help you finish well, as you go along make notes in the back of the book on *Key Experiences and Answers to Prayer that Built Your Hope.* After you finish Day 30 in your journal and your *Countdown to Hope* is finished, you will find a *Conclusion* page and a place to summarize *What I have learned and where I want to go from here.*

Hope endures to the end

Keep your eyes focused on the goal, as Jesus did. Jesus, "for the joy that was set before Him, endured the cross, despising the shame, and is set down at the right hand of the throne of God" (Hebrews 12:2 KJV). It takes endurance to go all the way to the cross, but that is where the joy is.

Remember these three from 1 Corinthians 13—faith, hope, and love. You need them now and you will need them later to finish your course with joy as you approach the time when you see God face to face.

Hope is the vision.

Love is the motivation.

Faith is the engine that drives you.

Section 2

Your Personal
Dare to Hope
Journal

DAYS 1-30 AND CONCLUSION

	A. THE TRUE MEANING OF HOPE
Day 1.	Hoping that God Accepts You *(Fanny Crosby)*
Day 2.	Hopeful Because God Values You *(William Booth)*
Day 3.	God's High Hopes for You *(Jonathan Edwards)*
Day 4.	God's Hope That You Will Be Like Jesus *(Hiram Revels)*
	B. BECOMING A HOPEFUL PERSON YOURSELF
Day 5.	Cultivating God's Presence to Release Hope *(George Fox)*
Day 6.	Building Hope From a Place of Humility *(Harriet Tubman)*
Day 7.	Commanding Your Soul to Hope *(Robert Smalls)*
Day 8.	Releasing Hope by Forgiveness *(Corrie ten Boom)*
Day 9.	Restoring Hope by Repentance *(James McGready)*
Day 10.	Increasing the Reach of Your Prayers by Hope *(John Knox)*
Day 11.	Hope for Financial Independence *(Maggie Walker)*
	C. HELPING OTHERS BY YOUR HOPE
Day 12.	Deciding to Have Hope for Others *(John Wesley)*
Day 13.	Uniting Families Through Hope *(Frederick Douglass)*
Day 14.	Sacrificing in Hopes of Others' Change *(Charles Finney)*
Day 15.	Hoping Your Donations Make a Difference *(Lewis Tappan)*
Day 16.	Sanctifying Yourself to Spread Hope *(Thomas Johnson)*
Day 17.	Hoping for a Harvest of Souls *(Charles Spurgeon)*
Day 18.	Changing Society by Hope *(William Wilberforce)*
Day 19.	Replenishing Hope of the Poor *(George Washington Carver)*
Day 20.	Praying for Hopeless Sinners *(Father Daniel Nash)*
Day 21.	Preaching Hope From a Warehouse *(William Seymour)*
Day 22.	Inspiring Hope by Writing *(Harriet Beecher Stowe)*
Day 23.	Sustaining Hope Under Fire *(John Calvin)*
Day 24.	Hoping to Be the Light of the World *(Francis Asbury)*
	D. HOPE AS AN ETERNAL QUALITY
Day 25.	Eternal Value of Hope *(David Brainerd)*
Day 26.	The Next Dimension of Hope *(Horatio Spafford)*
Day 27.	Ever-Increasing Hope *(D.L. Moody)*
Day 28.	The Splendor of Hope *(The Puritans)*
Day 29.	Hope of Eternal Life *(Catherine Booth)*
Day 30.	Hope of a Kingdom Under Christ *(Toccoa Falls Flood)*
Conclusion.	Where Will You Go From Here?

HOPING THAT GOD ACCEPTS YOU

"Blessed be the God and Father of our Lord Jesus Christ, who
has blessed us with every spiritual blessing in the heavenly
places in Christ, just as He chose us in Him before the
foundation of the world, that we should be holy and without
blame before Him in love, having predestined us to adoption as
sons by Jesus Christ to Himself, according to the good pleasure
of His will, to the praise of the glory of His grace, by which He
made us accepted in the Beloved" (Ephesians 1:3-6 NKJV).

Nothing can give you fulfillment or fill you with a personal sense of value like God's words of acceptance and saving grace: "You are accepted in the Beloved" (Ephesians 1:6 NKJV).

The Bible says that "it is God who works in you both to will and to do for His good pleasure" (Philippians 2:13 NKJV). When you are challenged with whether or not you should trust Him with your life, *let go and let God.* Even though you want to be in control and you struggle to understand first before you yield, just give up, give in, and say, "Yes, Lord. Fulfill your will in my life. I yield myself to you. Use me as I am."

God wants to use you now. He wants to be able to say to you, "Well done," while you are still alive and active in the earth. The Bible says to be absent from the body is to be present with the Lord (2 Corinthians 5:8) but don't wait until you are dead to be present with the Lord and hearing God's voice. You can hear Him clearly in *this* life—now—saying, "Well done, my good and faithful servant" (Matthew 25:21).

The degree to which you believe that God accepts you as you are is the degree to which you will seek His face and look into His eyes. All of your inner conflicts are resolved by the eyes of the Lord. Paul knew when his work was finished that he would receive a reward in heaven because he already knew that he was approved in God's sight on a daily basis. He knew that when He went to be with the Lord He would hear words of approval and acceptance. He would receive a crown.

All of us can live an approved life. You get approved by God in the closet of prayer, not from seeking honor and recognition by people.

As you wait for the Lord, keep your spirit right, humble yourself, and expect to be reproved, because God always reproves to improve. You cannot have a vital prayer life with God without being corrected. If you can't handle the correction of man, you can't touch the correction of God.

The Lord loves you. He speaks to you. He deals with the root issues in your life. He empowers you with hope that you can change and through your change you can be a blessing to Him and those around you.

THROUGH-THE-BIBLE IN ONE YEAR DAILY READING GUIDE
Fill in the four Bible chapters for today's date from the guide in the back of this journal.

Today's Four Bible Readings	My Personal Notes
❑ _____	_____
❑ _____	_____
❑ _____	_____
❑ _____	_____

MY PRAYER PRIORITIES FOR TODAY

My Right Relationship With God

_____
_____
_____
_____

Leaders—Local, State, Nation, World

_____
_____
_____
_____

Needs of Family and Friends

_____
_____
_____
_____

Worldwide Revivals and Awakenings

_____
_____
_____
_____

Five-Fold Ministry Church Leadership

_____
_____
_____
_____

Praise and Thanksgiving

_____
_____
_____
_____

"BLESSED ASSURANCE, JESUS IS MINE"

"Blessèd assurance, Jesus is mine!
O what a foretaste of glory divine!
Heir of salvation, purchase of God,
Born of His Spirit, washed in His blood.
This is my story, this is my song,
Praising my Savior, all the day long;
This is my story, this is my song,
Praising my Savior, all the day long."
—Fanny Crosby (1820-1915)

MONEY MANAGEMENT AND WEALTH

_____   _____
_____   _____
_____   _____
_____   _____

"I, the LORD, have called you to demonstrate my righteousness. I will guard and support you, for I have given you to my people as the personal confirmation of my covenant with them. And you will be a light to guide all nations to me. You will open the eyes of the blind and free the captives from prison. You will release those who sit in dark dungeons" (Isaiah 42:6-7).

MY TREASURE CHEST OF HOPE

Counting My Many Blessings   Planning My Hopes and Dreams

_____   _____
_____   _____
_____   _____
_____   _____
_____   _____
_____   _____
_____   _____

GREAT TESTIMONIES OF HOPE—FANNY CROSBY

Blindness could not stop her from writing songs

During Fanny Crosby's lifetime of nearly 95 years (1820-1915), she wrote more than 8,000 songs. She was blinded at six weeks of age by a medical error, but that did not stop her from becoming one of the most prolific hymn writers in history and one of the best known and well respected women of her era.

Although God was already using her, Fanny Crosby did not consider herself truly converted until she was 31 years old. She heard the hymn of another writer, Isaac Watts, which spoke of the humble state of man as a worm. She wrote, "After a prayer was offered, they began to sing the grand old consecration hymn, 'Alas! And Did My Saviour Bleed?' "

From then on, she loved and served Jesus Christ.

"Pass Me Not, O Gentle Savior" was her first song to gain worldwide attention. Like other poems, it began to stir inside of her as she heard the heart-rending cry of a sinner calling on God. She wrote it after hearing a prison inmate say, "O Lord, don't pass me by!"

During the 1875 Dwight L. Moody crusades in London, Ira Sankey sang the song every night because the crowds loved it so much. An alcoholic in the crowd heard it and whispered, "Oh, I wish He would not pass me by." When he returned the following night, the service began with that hymn, and he went forward and was saved. For the next forty years he carried a copy of the words until, as a successful businessman, he finally met Fanny Crosby.

SOME ACCOMPLISHMENTS OF FANNY CROSBY (1820-1915)

- *8,000 poems (song lyrics).* She wrote so many that sometimes she did not recognize the words when she heard one of her own songs.
- *200 pen names.* Publishers did not want the public to know she had written so many of their hymns.
- *Daily productivity.* Could write up to seven hymns in one day.
- *No copyrights.* Was paid only $1 or $2 for each poem and had no copyrights. The composers of the tunes usually kept all the rights.
- *Living simply.* In spite of the urging of friends and admirers, she chose to live among the poor.
- *Simplifying the Gospel.* She wrote for those who might not understand preaching and many were saved as a result.

Sample of song titles

- "Blessed Assurance, Jesus Is Mine"
- "He Hideth My Soul"
- "Near the Cross"
- "I Am Thine, O Lord"
- "To God Be the Glory"
- "Rescue the Perishing"

Fanny once said, "Mother, if I had a choice, I would still choose to remain blind . . . for when I die, the first face I will ever see will be the face of my blessed Saviour."

Are you excited about dying some day and seeing God's face? In that day, you will know what God has known about you all along. Will your face be full of joy at seeing Him face to face, or will you be distressed at how you failed Him?

The choice is yours.

24-HOUR PERSONAL ACCOUNTABILITY JOURNAL
How I spent every hour of my life today

12 AM	
1 AM	
2 AM	
3 AM	
4 AM	
5 AM	
6 AM	
7 AM	
8 AM	
9 AM	
10 AM	
11 AM	
12 PM	
1 PM	
2 PM	
3 PM	
4 PM	
5 PM	
6 PM	
7 PM	
8 PM	
9 PM	
10 PM	
11 PM	

TODAY'S JOURNAL OF PERSONAL INSIGHTS

_____

_____

_____

_____

_____

_____

_____

_____

_____

_____

_____

_____

_____

*"Then I saw thrones, and the people sitting on them
had been given the authority to judge" (Revelation 20:4).*

MY SELF-EVALUATION—HOW WELL DID I DO TODAY?

You may grade yourself as you rate your day. This is between you and God.

☐ Praise, worship, and thanksgiving   ☐ Family time

☐ Prayer and extraordinary prayer   ☐ Time with friends

☐ Reading and meditating on the Word of God   ☐ Reaching the lost

☐ Fasting and other sacrifices   ☐ Eating right and exercising

☐ Serving others in Christ-like love   ☐ Organizing myself to serve God

*"You have been chosen to know me, believe in me, and understand that I alone am
God. There is no other God; there never has been and never will be.
I am the LORD, and there is no other Savior" (Isaiah 43:10-11).*

Only 29 days to go in your *Countdown to Hope.*

HOPEFUL BECAUSE GOD VALUES YOU

"You are of God, little children" (1 John 4:4 NKJV).

E very person in the Bible traces his genealogy back to Adam, and Adam goes back to God. You could say that every human being—including you—traces his existence back to God Himself.

The fact that you exist today says more about God than it says about you. Your life is important to God because He created you and He still values your life. Your significance isn't based on your education or accomplishments. Those are insignificant compared to the value God places on you as His creation.

The greatest trick of the devil is to keep you in the dark about why God created you. The devil tries to steal your hope and tell you that your life has no meaning and is going nowhere, *but that is a lie.* Your coming days will be better than those that have gone before. You will fulfill a specific purpose that God had in mind when He made you. God values what you are becoming. You are His hope for the future. He wills you to live. You must not die until you fulfill His purposes for your life.

The New Testament says, "You are of God, little children." Christians who are in the dark don't understand that they are of God. When you know without a doubt that you are of God and you are a child of God, you will become a hopeful person. You will walk in light and see that your life has relevance to a future that your loving heavenly Father has planned.

Geographically speaking, both light and dark can exist at the same time. When it is dark in Atlanta, it can be daylight in South Africa, where my daughter lives. It's the same with you. Both darkness and light can exist in you at the same time, too. Maybe you are saved but in the dark about life. Why don't I have more money? Why don't people appreciate me? Why can't I find a mate? Why don't I have a better marriage?

You were made to walk in the light. Instead of being overtaken by questions and concerns, you can become a person of peace, wisdom, and understanding if you cultivate hope. If you have done dark things that have separated you from God, just say you're sorry. Everybody has to say "I'm sorry" to get to God. Confess and repent. Say, "I was wrong, please forgive me." Repentance keeps your hope alive.

What Jesus said on the cross applies to everyone who receives Him—"Father forgive them, for they know not what they do." Receive His forgiveness. Walk in the light of His hopes for you.

THROUGH-THE-BIBLE IN ONE YEAR DAILY READING GUIDE

Fill in the four Bible chapters for today's date from the guide in the back of this journal.

Today's Four Bible Readings	My Personal Notes
☐ _____	_____
☐ _____	_____
☐ _____	_____
☐ _____	_____

MY PRAYER PRIORITIES FOR TODAY

My Right Relationship With God

_____
_____
_____
_____

Leaders—Local, State, Nation, World

_____
_____
_____
_____

Needs of Family and Friends

_____
_____
_____
_____

Worldwide Revivals and Awakenings

_____
_____
_____
_____

Five-Fold Ministry Church Leadership

_____
_____
_____
_____

Praise and Thanksgiving

_____
_____
_____
_____

CHRISTIAN, YOU MUST NOT HOLD BACK!

"He still calls to you and bids to you to come. You must do it! You cannot hold back. You have enjoyed yourself in Christianity long enough."
—William Booth (1829-1912)

MONEY MANAGEMENT AND WEALTH

_____   _____
_____   _____
_____   _____
_____   _____

"Do not be afraid, for I have ransomed you. I have called you by name; you are mine. When you go through deep waters and great trouble, I will be with you"
(Isaiah 43:1-2).

MY TREASURE CHEST OF HOPE

Counting My Many Blessings   Planning My Hopes and Dreams

_____   _____
_____   _____
_____   _____
_____   _____
_____   _____
_____   _____
_____   _____

GREAT TESTIMONIES OF HOPE—WILLIAM BOOTH

Seeing society from God's perspective, not man's

William Booth (1829-1912), co-founder of the Salvation Army, saw great darkness in his day, but he didn't look to the government to bring the light. He looked for solutions from God's perspective, not man's.

In his book *In Darkest England and the Way Out,* he described desperate problems and also gave God's solutions. He issued a call for the best within each person to come forth to win the battle against evil.

He wrote in his book, "As in Africa streams intersect the forest in every direction, so the gin-shop stands at every corner with its River of the Water of Death flowing seventeen hours out of the twenty-four for the destruction of the people. A population sodden with drink, steeped in vice, eaten up by every social and physical malady, these are the denizens [inhabitants] of Darkest England amidst whom my life has been spent, and to whose rescue I would now summon all that is best in the manhood and womanhood of our land."

He described in detail not only the darkness—the despicable problems of his day—but also the light—the solutions that would come if more people could be saved. Booth was driven to help people not only to relieve their temporary suffering but also to make a way for them to find eternal life in Jesus Christ. He said, "But in providing for the relief of temporal misery I reckon that I am only making it easy where it is now difficult, and possible where it is now all but impossible, for men and women to find their way to the Cross of our Lord Jesus Christ."

When you read the challenge by William Booth that follows, it will either scare you to death or make you want to leave behind your comfortable Christianity and face boldly the dangers of true commitment.

"Does the surging sea look dark and dangerous?
Unquestionably it is so. There is no doubt that the leap
for you, as for everyone who takes it, means difficulty
and scorn and suffering. For you it may mean more than
this. It may mean death. He who beckons you from the
sea, however, knows what it will mean—and knowing,
He still calls to you and bids to you to come.
You must do it! You cannot hold back.
You have enjoyed yourself in Christianity long enough."

When William and Catherine Booth founded the Salvation Army in 1865, they set strong standards. Their people would be holy and unafraid to suffer for Christ's sake. They would go for God, regardless of the cost and humiliation. Most Christians I know make excuses for not speaking publicly about Christ, but not the Salvation Army. For more than a century they have been subjected to ridicule and persecution, but are so dedicated to rescuing sinners in His name that now the world comes to their door.

When God gives you a passion for souls, the church becomes a sending station instead of a resort location. Pastors no longer boast about how many people come to church on a Sunday morning but how many are sent out to spread the light of hope.

If the Church can change into the likeness of Jesus and fulfill the purpose of our creation, everything we do will function more like heaven on earth. Wherever we go we will take the light of hope that burns inside.

24-HOUR PERSONAL ACCOUNTABILITY JOURNAL
How I spent every hour of my life today

12 AM	
1 AM	
2 AM	
3 AM	
4 AM	
5 AM	
6 AM	
7 AM	
8 AM	
9 AM	
10 AM	
11 AM	
12 PM	
1 PM	
2 PM	
3 PM	
4 PM	
5 PM	
6 PM	
7 PM	
8 PM	
9 PM	
10 PM	
11 PM	

TODAY'S JOURNAL OF PERSONAL INSIGHTS

_____

_____

_____

_____

_____

_____

_____

_____

_____

_____

_____

"Happy are those whom you discipline, LORD,
and those whom you teach from your law" (Psalm 94:12).

MY SELF-EVALUATION—HOW WELL DID I DO TODAY?

You may grade yourself as you rate your day. This is between you and God.

❑ Praise, worship, and thanksgiving   ❑ Family time

❑ Prayer and extraordinary prayer   ❑ Time with friends

❑ Reading and meditating on the Word of God   ❑ Reaching the lost

❑ Fasting and other sacrifices   ❑ Eating right and exercising

❑ Serving others in Christ-like love   ❑ Organizing myself to serve God

"For the LORD your God is bringing you into a good land of flowing streams and
pools of water, with springs that gush forth in the valleys and hills"
(Deuteronomy 8:7).

Only 28 days to go in your *Countdown to Hope.*

DAY 3. _____ *(date)*

GOD'S HIGH HOPES FOR YOU

"And God said, Let us make man in our image, after our
likeness: and let them have dominion" (Genesis 1:26 KJV).
"And the LORD God said, 'It is not good for the man to be
alone' " (Genesis 2:18).

When God said that man would be created "in our image, after our likeness," He was giving away something of Himself to man. He was saying, "My perfection must be multiplied in My creation."

There is something great about God's creation of man—His creation of *you*—that relates to Who God is in heaven. Man is God's greatest hope, so God's hope is in you and what you become in Him.

First God said, "Let us create man in Our image, after Our likeness." Then He went on to define man's purpose—dominion over the whole earth. Your creation relates to God's future plans for the earth—the dominion of people who are just like Him taking responsibility over His creation. When you don't fulfill His hopes for you, His plan is hindered.

When God said that it was not good that man should be alone, His statement came from a value that God held Himself, so in effect God was saying, "It is not good that *I* should be alone." If it was not good that *man* should be alone, it was not good that *God* should be alone, either.

The idea that our relationship with God is a fulfillment of God's hope that He would not be alone requires a significant shift in our thinking. We don't usually consider how God thinks. We pray about what we need and what we want God to do for us, but we don't consider what God needs.

God will not be forced into answering a prayer that will negatively affect His ultimate plans or contradict His standards. He does what He wants based on His all-knowing view, not our limited perspective.

Sometimes God allows things that are not in His best interests or ours, either. For example, He allowed Israel to have a king. However, He had already thought about how he would fix it later. King Saul was the fulfillment of God's warnings, but David was a king after God's own heart.

The troubles that you see on earth have resulted because God's permissive will allowed man in his fallen nature to do what he wanted, but God is not through with us yet. All of the great things that God still wants to do will come to pass when you and I decide to do what God wants. We are God's great hope for the future. When we respond to His call for fellowship and accountability, He will entrust us with more of His plans.

THROUGH-THE-BIBLE IN ONE YEAR DAILY READING GUIDE

Read the four Bible chapters for today's date from the Through-the-Bible Reading Guide in the back of this journal. Make any additional notes here.

Today's Bible Readings | My Personal Notes

❑ _____   _____

❑ _____   _____

❑ _____   _____

❑ _____   _____

MY PRAYER PRIORITIES FOR TODAY

My Right Relationship With God

_____
_____
_____

Leaders—Local, State, Nation, World

_____
_____
_____

Needs of Family and Friends

_____
_____
_____

Worldwide Revivals and Awakenings

_____
_____
_____

Five-Fold Ministry Church Leadership

_____
_____
_____

Praise and Thanksgiving

_____
_____
_____

A DOOR OF HOPE

"God is wont to open a door of hope, a door through which there flashes a sweet light out of heaven upon the soul. Then comfort arises, and then is there a new song in the mouth, even praise unto God." —Jonathan Edwards (1703-1758)

MONEY MANAGEMENT AND WEALTH

_____   _____
_____   _____
_____   _____
_____   _____

"The LORD looks down from heaven and sees the whole human race.
From his throne he observes all who live on the earth.
He made their hearts, so he understands everything they do" (Psalm 33:13-15).

MY TREASURE CHEST OF HOPE

Counting My Many Blessings   Planning My Hopes and Dreams

_____   _____
_____   _____
_____   _____
_____   _____
_____   _____
_____   _____
_____   _____

GREAT TESTIMONIES OF HOPE—JONATHAN EDWARDS

His teenage daughter's death could not destroy his hope

When 18th century missionary David Brainerd was dying from tuberculosis, the teenage daughter of Jonathan Edwards, Jerusha, became his nurse. She and Brainerd had once considered marriage, but decided instead that he would dedicate himself to the Native Americans.

Four months after Brainerd's death, Jerusha died, also. Edwards was such a man of hope and faith that he accepted the death of his daughter and continued to thank God publicly that Brainerd's brief life had been a divine inspiration to him.

He wrote that "it has pleased a holy and sovereign God to take away this my dear child by death, on the fourteenth of February, next following; after a short illness of five days, in the eighteenth year of her age. She was a person of much the same spirit with Mr. Brainerd. She had constantly taken care of and attended him in his sickness for nineteen weeks before his death, devoting herself to it with great delight because she looked on him as an eminent servant of Jesus Christ."

Edwards was a truly remarkable man. He was a pastor who not only helped spark America's First Great Awakening and himself ministered to the Native Americans in later years, but was also a prolific writer and is considered America's greatest theologian.

LIFE OF JONATHAN EDWARDS (1703-1758)

- Entered Yale before 13th birthday, graduating four years later at head of his class.

- In 1729, succeeded his grandfather, Solomon Stoddard, as pastor of the prestigious Congregational Church in Northampton, Massachusetts.

- In 1734, six people were suddenly converted in his church, then 30 or more every week. America's First Great Awakening was launched.

- In 1741, preached the famous sermon "Sinners in the Hands of an Angry God" at Enfield, Connecticut. Even though his preaching style was not dramatic, the power of God was so strong that parishioners screamed and held onto the pillars of the church, fearing they would fall into hell.

- Wrote numerous scholarly works and is considered America's greatest theologian.

  He explained history as God's work structured around
  His scriptural promises, interspersed by
  periods of the outpouring of His Spirit.

- Edited journal of David Brainerd, a missionary to Native Americans who died at the Edwards' home at the age of 29. This journal is credited with inspiring some of the greatest evangelists and missionaries in history.

- In 1750, he was removed as pastor of the Northampton church because of his commitment to godly standards for church members and his requirement of proof that members were truly saved.

- From 1751-1757, he served in Stockbridge, Massachusetts, where he ministered to Native Americans.

- In 1757, he became president of the College of New Jersey, now Princeton, but died a few months later from smallpox.

His descendants for generations were pastors, judges, college presidents, and elected officials—men and women of great accomplishment. Their success was built on the foundation of hope in God.

24-HOUR PERSONAL ACCOUNTABILITY JOURNAL
How I spent every hour of my life today

12 AM	
1 AM	
2 AM	
3 AM	
4 AM	
5 AM	
6 AM	
7 AM	
8 AM	
9 AM	
10 AM	
11 AM	
12 PM	
1 PM	
2 PM	
3 PM	
4 PM	
5 PM	
6 PM	
7 PM	
8 PM	
9 PM	
10 PM	
11 PM	

TODAY'S JOURNAL OF PERSONAL INSIGHTS

_____
_____
_____
_____
_____
_____
_____
_____
_____
_____

The Bible says we are to judge ourselves. The Greek word translated "judge" in 1 Corinthians 11:31 (KJV) is diakrino. *It means to discern or to separate thoroughly, to discriminate and decide.*

MY SELF-EVALUATION—HOW WELL DID I DO TODAY?

You may grade yourself as you rate your day. This is between you and God.

❏ Praise, worship, and thanksgiving   ❏ Family time

❏ Prayer and extraordinary prayer   ❏ Time with friends

❏ Reading and meditating on the Word of God   ❏ Reaching the lost

❏ Fasting and other sacrifices   ❏ Eating right and exercising

❏ Serving others in Christ-like love   ❏ Organizing myself to serve God

" 'Look, I am making all things new!' And then he said to me, 'Write this down, for what I tell you is trustworthy and true' " (Revelation 21:5).

Only 27 days to go in your Countdown to Hope.

GOD'S HOPE THAT YOU WILL BE LIKE JESUS

*"For God knew his people in advance, and he chose them to
become like his Son, so that his Son would be the firstborn,
with many brothers and sisters. And having chosen them, he
called them to come to him. And he gave them right standing
with himself, and he promised them his glory"
(Romans 8:29-30).*

If God hasn't lost His hope, you shouldn't lose your hope. Hope is the
goal. God's hope is you. When God made man, the ultimate being of His
creation, He said, "Let us make man in our image and after our likeness."
God's image and likeness were in heaven. The last thing thrown out of
heaven was bound in chains. Everything left behind in heaven was in a
divine flow, but God said it is not enough. "I am the God of expansion. I
am the God of eternity. I am the God of the end and the beginning."

God said, "I am going to make a man in My image and after My
likeness. I know that I already have hope in Myself. I see the end from the
beginning. I am going to make a man so that My hope can be expressed in
the earth as well as in heaven. I will not only have hope in Myself. I will
put My hope in the man I created and no matter what he does I am not
going to give up hope in him. My hope has now been transferred into a
man whom I chose to make in My image after My likeness."

God gave Himself for mankind. In the New Testament it says,
"Husbands, love your wives, even as Christ also loved the church, and
gave himself for it" (Ephesians 5:25 KJV). God puts His greatest value in
the one He has hopes for. God never gives up hope in you. He ever lives to
make intercession for you. It doesn't matter how you feel about yourself.
Jesus is still praying. Whatever you have done wrong, Jesus is still your
advocate. Whatever your circumstances, God has plans for you.

The will of God has intersected with the will of man and God's
will is winning over your life. God s hope is the dominating aspect of what
is going on in your life. Even when you can't see it, "we know that God
causes everything to work together for the good of those who love God and
are called according to his purpose for them" (Romans 8:28).

The Bible says that when someone is born of God the love of God
dwells in him. You have the love of God in your nature and the right
motivation in your inner man. You may not feel like it. You may not think
like it. You may not look like it, but the right motivation is inside. The God
of hope isn't finished with you yet. God is still working on you right now.

THROUGH-THE-BIBLE IN ONE YEAR DAILY READING GUIDE

Fill in the four Bible chapters for today's date from the guide in the back of this journal.

Today's Four Bible Readings	My Personal Notes
☐ _____	_____
☐ _____	_____
☐ _____	_____
☐ _____	_____

MY PRAYER PRIORITIES FOR TODAY

My Right Relationship With God

_____
_____
_____

Leaders—Local, State, Nation, World

_____
_____
_____

Needs of Family and Friends

_____
_____
_____

Worldwide Revivals and Awakenings

_____
_____
_____

Five-Fold Ministry Church Leadership

_____
_____
_____

Praise and Thanksgiving

_____
_____
_____

AMERICA WON'T PROSPER WHILE PREJUDICE REMAINS

""I find that the prejudice in this country to color is very great, and I sometimes fear that it is on the increase. . . . If the nation should take a step for the encouragement of this prejudice against the colored race, can they have any grounds upon which to predicate a hope that Heaven will smile upon them and prosper them?"—U.S. Senator Hiram Revels (1827-1901).

MONEY MANAGEMENT AND WEALTH

_____   _____
_____   _____
_____   _____
_____   _____

"I have called you back from the ends of the earth so you can serve me. For I have chosen you and will not throw you away. Don't be afraid, for I am with you. Do not be dismayed, for I am your God. I will strengthen you. I will help you. I will uphold you with my victorious right hand" (Isaiah 41:9-10).

MY TREASURE CHEST OF HOPE

Counting My Many Blessings   Planning My Hopes and Dreams

_____   _____
_____   _____
_____   _____
_____   _____
_____   _____
_____   _____
_____   _____

GREAT TESTIMONIES OF HOPE—BLACKS IN RECONSTRUCTION

Hoping for equality, serving with distinction

Slavery was included in the U.S. Constitution and dominated the Constitution of the Confederacy. Most of the early U.S. presidents bought and sold human beings, even as they spoke publicly about "unalienable rights" and the need to end slavery. With the passage of years, some of these presidents have even won admiration for how nicely they treated their slaves. But what was the enduring impact? How much of slavery's influence persisted for centuries and still has an impact today?

The first Black to serve in the U.S. Congress was Hiram Rhodes Revels (1827-1901) of Mississippi. He had been born free in North Carolina and became a minister in the African Methodist Episcopal Church. He established a school for freedmen in St. Louis, Missouri.

After the outbreak of the Civil War, he assisted in recruiting Blacks into the military and served as a chaplain.

After the war was over, Revels was serving as a state senator from Mississippi when he was chosen to fill the unexpired term for the U.S. Senate seat formerly held by Albert Brown before Mississippi seceded from the Union. The other senate seat had been held by Jefferson Davis, who became president of the Confederacy.

One of Revel's colleagues, John Lynch, the first Black speaker of the House in Mississippi and a member of the U. S. House of Representatives, wrote in *The Facts of Reconstruction* about the power of Revel's prayer opening the Mississippi legislature in January 1870:

> *"That prayer,—one of the most impressive and eloquent prayers that had ever been delivered in the Senate Chamber,—made Revels a United States Senator. He made a profound impression upon all who heard him. It impressed those who heard it that Revels was not only a man of great natural ability but that he was also a man of superior attainments."*

Revels began his term on February 25, 1870, two days after Mississippi was readmitted to the Union. Before he was seated, however, Democratic members challenged his credentials, claiming he had only been a citizen since the passage of the 14th Amendment. Republican senators supported him and several days later on a 48 to 8 vote he was seated as the first Black U.S. Senator.

Senator James Blaine of Maine (1830-1893), who was White, wrote in his book *Twenty Years of Congress* about the character of his Black colleagues who came into office during Reconstruction:

> *"The colored men who took seats in both Senate and House did not appear ignorant or helpless. They were as a rule studious, earnest, ambitious men, whose public conduct—as illustrated by Mr. Revels and Mr. Bruce in the Senate, and by Mr. Rapier, Mr. Lynch and Mr. Rainey in the House—would be honorable to any race. Coals of fire were heaped on the heads of all their enemies when the colored men in Congress heartily joined in removing the disabilities of those who had before been their oppressors, and who, with deep regret be it said, have continued to treat them with injustice and ignominy."*

All during slavery, I believe that God had His eye on Black Christian men who would some day have an opportunity to represent the character of Christ in Congress. What does He have in mind for you?

24-HOUR PERSONAL ACCOUNTABILITY JOURNAL
How I spent every hour of my life today

12 AM	
1 AM	
2 AM	
3 AM	
4 AM	
5 AM	
6 AM	
7 AM	
8 AM	
9 AM	
10 AM	
11 AM	
12 PM	
1 PM	
2 PM	
3 PM	
4 PM	
5 PM	
6 PM	
7 PM	
8 PM	
9 PM	
10 PM	
11 PM	

TODAY'S JOURNAL OF PERSONAL INSIGHTS

_____

_____

_____

_____

_____

_____

_____

_____

_____

_____

_____

"Who is a faithful, sensible servant, to whom the master can give the responsibility of managing his household and feeding his family? If the master returns and finds that the servant has done a good job, there will be a reward. I assure you, the master will put that servant in charge of all he owns" (Matthew 24:45-47).

MY SELF-EVALUATION—HOW WELL DID I DO TODAY?
You may grade yourself as you rate your day. This is between you and God.

❏ Praise, worship, and thanksgiving   ❏ Family time

❏ Prayer and extraordinary prayer   ❏ Time with friends

❏ Reading and meditating on the Word of God   ❏ Reaching the lost

❏ Fasting and other sacrifices   ❏ Eating right and exercising

❏ Serving others in Christ-like love   ❏ Organizing myself to serve God

" 'I am the Alpha and the Omega—the beginning and the end,' says the Lord God. 'I am the one who is, who always was, and who is still to come, the Almighty One' " (Revelation 1:8).

Only 26 days to go in your *Countdown to Hope.*

CULTIVATING GOD'S PRESENCE TO RELEASE HOPE

"Yet I still dare to hope when I remember this:
The unfailing love of the LORD never ends! By his mercies we
have been kept from complete destruction. Great is his
faithfulness; his mercies begin afresh each day. I say to myself,
'The LORD is my inheritance; therefore, I will hope in him!' "
(Lamentations 3:21-24).

In the midst of writing down his sorrows in the passage above, Jeremiah stopped himself and said, "When I remember. . . ." There was still some hope left in his memory bank. Before that, he said, "I remember everything bad," but then he began thinking about who God is and he remembered the good. The devil tries hard to destroy your memories of God's goodness to make your need seem greater than God's provision, but God has done so much for you that you can't even count it all. When you remember your circumstances, bad thoughts dominate you, but when you remember how great God is, the good dominates. That is when hope comes alive.

Jeremiah listed five things he remembered that activated his hope:

1. *The unfailing love of the Lord never ends.*

2. *By His mercies I have been kept from complete destruction.*

3. *Great is His faithfulness.*

4. *His mercies begin afresh every day.*

5. *I say hopeful things to myself. I speak hope into my own mind.*

When you understand that God is with you and His love never fails, you are grateful that you are no longer consumed by the bad things in your life. You forget it all and celebrate God's goodness. You are filled with hope. You acknowledge, "Lord, you are keeping me right now in ways that I don't understand. God, I am so sorry for accusing you falsely."

With all of your challenges, dare to hope! As the old mothers would say, *"I dare you to have hope! I double-dog dare you to have hope!"* Even if all else is gone and you have nothing left, God is there. He is not discouraged about anything. He sees the end from the beginning. He knows the way ahead and it will all turn out for the best.

Celebrate the renewal of hope every morning. You might even sing songs like "Great Is Thy Faithfulness, O God My Father," which is based on Lamentations 3.

Whenever you need Him most, God will be there with hope.

THROUGH-THE-BIBLE IN ONE YEAR DAILY READING GUIDE

Fill in the four Bible chapters for today's date from the guide in the back of this journal.

Today's Four Bible Readings	My Personal Notes
❑ _____	_____
❑ _____	_____
❑ _____	_____
❑ _____	_____

MY PRAYER PRIORITIES FOR TODAY

My Right Relationship With God

_____
_____
_____

Leaders—Local, State, Nation, World

_____
_____
_____

Needs of Family and Friends

_____
_____
_____

Worldwide Revivals and Awakenings

_____
_____
_____

Five-Fold Ministry Church Leadership

_____
_____
_____

Praise and Thanksgiving

_____
_____
_____

OVERTAKEN BY THE LOVE OF GOD

"One day, when I had been walking solitarily abroad, and was come home, I was taken up in the love of God, so that I could not but admire the greatness of His love;. . . that all these troubles were good for me, and temptations for the trial of my faith, which Christ had given me." —George Fox (1624-1691)

MONEY MANAGEMENT AND WEALTH

_____   _____
_____   _____
_____   _____
_____   _____
_____   _____

"Then his people will live there undisturbed, for he will be highly honored all around the world. And he will be the source of our peace" (Micah 5:4-5).

MY TREASURE CHEST OF HOPE

Counting My Many Blessings   Planning My Hopes and Dreams

_____   _____
_____   _____
_____   _____
_____   _____
_____   _____
_____   _____
_____   _____
_____   _____

GREAT TESTIMONIES OF HOPE—GEORGE FOX

The inner presence of God

The Quakers, or "The Religious Society of Friends," was founded in the seventeenth century through the ministry of the Englishman George Fox (1624-1691). The name "Quakers" arose when the people who came to mock him were so convicted by his preaching that they began to quake in fear of God's eternal judgment.

Fox's spiritual inheritance came through godly parents who were Puritans. From a young age, he believed in Jesus Christ and was a seeker after God. A turning point in his life came with what he later called an "opening" or what I might call open heavens, when God is speaking to you and you are open to receive. Here is what he said:

"One day, when I had been walking solitarily abroad, and was come home, I was taken up in the love of God, so that I could not but admire the greatness of His love; and while I was in that condition, it was opened unto me by the eternal light and power, and I therein clearly saw that all was done and to be done in and by Christ, and how He conquers and destroys this tempter the devil, and all his works, and is atop of him; and that all these troubles were good for me, and temptations for the trial of my faith, which Christ had given me. The Lord opened me, that I saw all through these troubles and temptations. My living faith was raised, that I saw all was done by Christ the life, and my belief was in Him."

Divine revelation affects people differently. With Fox, it gave him a holy boldness and a righteous indignation at the hypocrisy and formalism of the churches. Like John the Baptist, he dressed in unorthodox clothes—a suit of leather—and began to proclaim divine judgment, even at the doors of other churches on Sunday mornings to startled parishioners.

That was a time in history when people were deathly serious about the Christian religion. Wars were fought and kings and queens rose and were deposed and even killed over different interpretations. As a result, George Fox and later many of his followers were put in jail for what they believed, but that did not stop them, because God was with them.

One of the distinguishing marks of the Quakers was the belief that each person can have a personal relationship with Jesus Christ. Regardless of his station in life, he can hear the Spirit of God speaking to him.

Today when they meet they set aside time to sit together quietly to hear God's voice. They approach God with reverence and fear.

When the movement spread to America through William Penn (founder of Pennsylvania), and others, some Quakers took great risks to save the lives of slaves escaping through the Underground Railroad.

In Harriet Beecher Stowe's anti-slavery novel *Uncle Tom's Cabin* she described how the Quakers' extraordinary Christian character changed the heart of a bitter escaped slave with "the light of a living Gospel, breathed in living faces, preached by a thousand unconscious acts of love and good will, which, like the cup of cold water given in the name of a disciple, shall never lose their reward."

Would you be willing to die for the right to serve and spread the Gospel like that?

24-HOUR PERSONAL ACCOUNTABILITY JOURNAL
How I spent every hour of my life today

12 AM	
1 AM	
2 AM	
3 AM	
4 AM	
5 AM	
6 AM	
7 AM	
8 AM	
9 AM	
10 AM	
11 AM	
12 PM	
1 PM	
2 PM	
3 PM	
4 PM	
5 PM	
6 PM	
7 PM	
8 PM	
9 PM	
10 PM	
11 PM	

TODAY'S JOURNAL OF PERSONAL INSIGHTS

_____

_____

_____

_____

_____

_____

_____

_____

_____

_____

*"And it is good for the young to submit to the yoke of his discipline.
Let them sit alone in silence beneath the LORD's demands" (Lamentations 3:27-28).*

MY SELF-EVALUATION—HOW WELL DID I DO TODAY?

You may grade yourself as you rate your day. This is between you and God.

❏ Praise, worship, and thanksgiving   ❏ Family time

❏ Prayer and extraordinary prayer   ❏ Time with friends

❏ Reading and meditating on the Word of God ❏ Reaching the lost

❏ Fasting and other sacrifices   ❏ Eating right and exercising

❏ Serving others in Christ-like love   ❏ Organizing myself to serve God

*"The LORD is wonderfully good to those who wait for him and seek him.
So it is good to wait quietly for salvation from the Lord" (Lamentations 3:25-26).*

Only 25 days to go in your *Countdown to Hope.*

DAY 6. _____ *(date)*

BUILDING HOPE FROM A PLACE OF HUMILITY

*"I pray that you will begin to understand the incredible
greatness of his power for us who believe him.
This is the same mighty power that raised Christ from the dead
and seated him in the place of honor at
God's right hand in the heavenly realms" (Ephesians 1:19-20).*

Your hope for the future has no limits when you humble yourself and acknowledge the greatness of God's power. When you see Him as King, high and lifted up, He Himself becomes your hope, because He is the great Creator of everything—seen and unseen—including you.

The Bible says that we put on Christ (Galatians 3:27). When you put on Christ, you receive Him as your Lord and Savior and your hope. In the face of His holiness, you see your own shameful behavior and say, "I am so sorry. Please forgive me, Lord." You hope in His forgiveness. When you recognize that there have been times when you have blamed God when He was actually at work on your problem and you just didn't know it, you hope He will trust you again.

Every need you have is met at the level of your relationship with God. You need to develop that relationship more than anything else you are doing in your life, and the way to grow in closeness to God is humility.

When Christ does something for a person who has humbled himself and submitted to His will, He is doing it for Himself because a humble person doesn't live for himself. He lives for God. In meeting your need, He is meeting His own need, but you can't see that until you realize that Christ Himself is your inheritance, and you are His.

You are the hope of God. When you and God connect, you go from glory to glory, from strength to strength, from faith to faith. You are someone whom God has called to fulfill His will. The Lord has declared that He will return for a glorious church that has not spot or wrinkle or any such thing but shall be holy and without blemish (Ephesians 5:27). He hopes that you will be among that number, living a sinless life, seeking to please Him daily.

The Spirit of God knows your infirmities better than you do. The plans He has for you are way beyond your ability, but He will bring those things to fulfillment. Keep walking in supernatural hope and you will be included in that number of God's people who are holy and without blemish—His people, fully satisfied and full of hope in every area of life.

THROUGH-THE-BIBLE IN ONE YEAR DAILY READING GUIDE

Fill in the four Bible chapters for today's date from the guide in the back of this journal.

Today's Four Bible Readings	My Personal Notes
❏ _____	_____
❏ _____	_____
❏ _____	_____
❏ _____	_____

MY PRAYER PRIORITIES FOR TODAY

My Right Relationship With God
_____
_____
_____
_____

Leaders—Local, State, Nation, World
_____
_____
_____
_____

Needs of Family and Friends
_____
_____
_____
_____

Worldwide Revivals and Awakenings
_____
_____
_____
_____

Five-Fold Ministry Church Leadership
_____
_____
_____
_____

Praise and Thanksgiving
_____
_____
_____
_____

HOLDING STEADY ON GOD FOR THE SAKE OF OTHERS

" 'But I was free, and they should be free. I would make a home in the North and bring them there, God helping me. Oh, how I prayed then,' she said; 'I said to de Lord, "I'm gwine to hole stiddy on to you, an' I know you'll see me through." ' "
—Harriet Tubman (c.1820-1913) about her miraculous escape from slavery

Money Management and Wealth

_____
_____   _____
_____   _____
_____   _____
_____   _____

"And not only so, but we glory in tribulations also: knowing that tribulation worketh patience; And patience, experience; and experience, hope: And hope maketh not ashamed; because the love of God is shed abroad in our hearts by the Holy Ghost which is given unto us" (Romans 5:3-5 KJV).

My Treasure Chest of Hope

Counting My Many Blessings   Planning My Hopes and Dreams

Great Testimonies of Hope—Harriet Tubman

Lord, sweep my heart clean

Harriet Tubman (c.1820-1913) was a field slave on Maryland's Eastern Shore when she escaped to freedom in 1849. During the next several years, she returned many times and miraculously led approximately 300 slaves to freedom. Even though there was a bounty on her head, she was never captured and never lost one of those she was rescuing.

However, before this happened, she learned the power of God through humility. On the next page is an excerpt from an account of her life as a slave by her biographer, Sarah Bradford.

" 'And so,' she said, 'from Christmas till March I worked as I could, and I prayed through all the long nights—I groaned and prayed for ole master: "Oh Lord, convert master!" "Oh Lord, change dat man's heart!" 'Pears like I prayed all de time,' said Harriet; ' 'bout my work, everywhere, I prayed an' I groaned to de Lord.

" 'When I went to de horse-trough to wash my face, I took up de water in my han' an' I said, "Oh Lord, wash me, make me clean!" Den I take up something to wipe my face, an' I say, "Oh Lord, wipe away all my sin!" When I took de broom and began to sweep, I groaned, "Oh Lord, wha'soebber sin dere be in my heart, sweep it out, Lord, clar an' clean!" '

"No words can describe the pathos of her tones, as she broke out into these words of prayer, after the manner of her people.

" 'An' so,' said she, 'I prayed all night long for master, till the first of March; an' all the time he was bringing people to look at me, an' trying to sell me. Den we heard dat some of us was gwine to be sole to go wid de chain-gang down to de cotton an' rice fields, and dey said I was gwine, an' my brudders, an' sisters. Den I changed my prayer. . . . I began to pray, "Oh Lord, if you ant nebber gwine to change dat man's heart, kill him, Lord, an' take him out ob de way."

" 'Nex' ting I heard old master was dead, an' he died jus' as he libed. Oh, then, it 'peared like I'd give all de world full ob gold, if I had it, to bring dat poor soul back. But I couldn't pray for him no longer.' "

In her lifetime, Harriet Tubman passed hundreds of times through the secret network called the Underground Railroad, guided by the unseen hand of God Who honored her integrity and humble faith.

24-HOUR PERSONAL ACCOUNTABILITY JOURNAL
How I spent every hour of my life today

12 AM	
1 AM	
2 AM	
3 AM	
4 AM	
5 AM	
6 AM	
7 AM	
8 AM	
9 AM	
10 AM	
11 AM	
12 PM	
1 PM	
2 PM	
3 PM	
4 PM	
5 PM	
6 PM	
7 PM	
8 PM	
9 PM	
10 PM	
11 PM	

TODAY'S JOURNAL OF PERSONAL INSIGHTS

_____

_____

_____

_____

_____

_____

_____

_____

_____

_____

_____

"For the time is come that judgment must begin at the house of God"
(1 Peter 4:17 KJV).

MY SELF-EVALUATION—HOW WELL DID I DO TODAY?

You may grade yourself as you rate your day. This is between you and God.

❑ Praise, worship, and thanksgiving   ❑ Family time

❑ Prayer and extraordinary prayer   ❑ Time with friends

❑ Reading and meditating on the Word of God ❑ Reaching the lost

❑ Fasting and other sacrifices   ❑ Eating right and exercising

❑ Serving others in Christ-like love   ❑ Organizing myself to serve God

". . . for the LORD is your security.
He will keep your foot from being caught in a trap" (Proverbs 3:26).

Only 24 days to go in your *Countdown to Hope.*

COMMANDING YOUR SOUL TO HOPE

"Why are you cast down, O my soul?
And why are you disquieted within me?
Hope in God, for I shall yet praise Him
For the help of His countenance"
(Psalm 42:5 NKJV).

David asked what we might call a rhetorical question: "Why art thou cast down, O my soul?" In other words, why are you so hopeless? Then he took command of his soul by a demand of submission. He said to his soul, "Hope in God!" Then by an act of his will he took an action step. He added, "I shall yet praise Him for the help of His countenance."

Praise affects your countenance—the way you look and the way you carry yourself. When you look in the face of God and see that the solution to all your problems is in Him, your load gets lighter. Your face begins to glow.

Discouragement and hopelessness affect the way you look, too— in a negative way. You walk in a dark cloud because you lack the assurance that God is with you. You allow yourself to get down because you forgot prosperity, as Jeremiah said (Lamentations 3:17).

Despair is not the picture that God wants to see when He looks at you. Sometimes your spirit has to make it clear to your emotions that they will not rule you. Your mental state will not rule you. The carnality of your flesh will not rule you. Your spirit is in charge and it's full of hope!

Some people always wear a happy face even when they are going through things. They never lose the ability to smile. Those people have learned how to control their souls. They have a prophetic grace on them. They take seriously the assurance that God is with them and that gives them hope. They don't let negative things come in and take control.

The battle for your soul takes place in the eternal realm. Every time that you take a stand against dark forces in your mind, will, and emotions you are growing closer to Christ-likeness.

The devil tries to convince you that you can't trust the living God! You have to tell him off and declare that you will trust the Lord and have faith in His holy name. You say, "I hope in God. My hope is renewed. I have a testimony of God's goodness in my life. I praise Him for His greatness toward me!"

When you win the battle for your soul, hope comes alive. You walk consistently in hope as you walk with God.

Through-the-Bible in One Year Daily Reading Guide

Fill in the four Bible chapters for today's date from the guide in the back of this journal.

Today's Four Bible Readings	My Personal Notes
❑ _____	_____
❑ _____	_____
❑ _____	_____
❑ _____	_____

My Prayer Priorities for Today

My Right Relationship With God

_____
_____
_____

Leaders—Local, State, Nation, World

_____
_____
_____

Needs of Family and Friends

_____
_____
_____

Worldwide Revivals and Awakenings

_____
_____
_____

Five-Fold Ministry Church Leadership

_____
_____
_____

Praise and Thanksgiving

_____
_____
_____

Take Us to Freedom

""Oh Lord, we entrust ourselves into thy hands.
Like thou didst for the Israelites in Egypt,
Please stand over us to our promised land of freedom."
—Robert Smalls (1839-1915), a slave, praying as he escaped with a Confederate ship

MONEY MANAGEMENT AND WEALTH

_____   _____
_____   _____
_____   _____
_____   _____

"So God has given us both his promise and his oath.
These two things are unchangeable because it is impossible for God to lie.
Therefore, we who have fled to him for refuge can take new courage,
for we can hold on to his promise with confidence" (Hebrews 6:18).

MY TREASURE CHEST OF HOPE

Counting My Many Blessings   Planning My Hopes and Dreams

_____   _____
_____   _____
_____   _____
_____   _____
_____   _____
_____   _____
_____   _____
_____   _____

GREAT TESTIMONIES OF HOPE—ROBERT SMALLS

Slave taking command of enemy ship helps shorten Civil War

In 1873, the people of South Carolina elected a former slave
named Robert Smalls (1839-1915) as a member of the U.S. House of
Representatives where he served from 1875-1886. He compiled a brilliant
record, served on several Congressional committees, and was known as a
powerful orator.

While Smalls was still in slavery, he became a hero by taking
command of the Confederate ship *Planter* and piloting it out of Charleston
harbor and into Union territory while the ship's captain and crew members
were ashore. Before he left the Confederate harbor with the ship, he
bravely picked up his wife and three children, also slaves, and sailed away
to freedom with his eight Black crew members.

Smalls knew the right signals to pass out of the port right under the noses of the Confederate sentries. At daybreak, safely out of reach, he raised the Stars and Stripes and surrendered himself and the ship into Union hands. Smalls provided the Union with invaluable intelligence concerning Confederate forts and encampments and was later chosen to pilot the ship for them.

Blacks like Smalls who were elected after the Civil War had to face obstacles that we cannot imagine today. For example, when Woodrow Wilson was elected as President of the United States, he betrayed Blacks like W.E.B. DuBois who helped him get elected and segregated all government offices. It was the first time some departments had been segregated since 1863, when Lincoln desegregated them. It was also a break with the civil service code that previous Presidents had set in place. Protestors were fired. When a Black delegation went to ask President Wilson to reverse his policies, he was rude and hostile and threw them out.

One of the Blacks removed from a federal office position in Wilson's purge was Robert Smalls. Smalls had been appointed by President William McKinley to the post of customs collector in Beaufort, South Carolina, in 1889, and he served for many years before the unjustified Wilson purge.

Smalls had received a reward for piloting the Planter out of Charleston harbor and with some of the reward money he purchased the house where he and his mother had been slaves and moved in.

One day, the wife of his former master, Mrs. McKee, came by the house that he now owned. She was elderly and somewhat confused, and still thought that it was her house. Instead of turning her away, Smalls brought her in and gave her back the bedroom that had been hers when she was his mistress and he was a slave, then served her.

Smalls died in 1915 at the age of 76, much honored. In 2001 the Army launched a Logistics Support Vessel (LSV-8) named the *Major General Robert Smalls*, the first ship named after a Black American.

You can recall the success of Smalls in commanding that enemy vessel when your soul becomes an enemy to your hope. Command your soul like an enemy ship. Say, as David did, "Hope in God!" Your rewards will be great. You will be able to serve your fellow man as a former slave to sin who has now discovered the truth and escaped. When persecutors come to disrupt your triumph, leave that to God and continue on in godliness.

24-HOUR PERSONAL ACCOUNTABILITY JOURNAL
How I spent every hour of my life today

12 AM	
1 AM	
2 AM	
3 AM	
4 AM	
5 AM	
6 AM	
7 AM	
8 AM	
9 AM	
10 AM	
11 AM	
12 PM	
1 PM	
2 PM	
3 PM	
4 PM	
5 PM	
6 PM	
7 PM	
8 PM	
9 PM	
10 PM	
11 PM	

TODAY'S JOURNAL OF PERSONAL INSIGHTS

_____

_____

_____

_____

_____

_____

_____

_____

_____

_____

_____

_____

_____

"May your gracious Spirit lead me forward on a firm footing. For the glory of your name, O LORD, save me. In your righteousness, bring me out of this distress. In your unfailing love, cut off all my enemies and destroy all my foes, for I am your servant" (Psalm 143:10-12).

MY SELF-EVALUATION—HOW WELL DID I DO TODAY?

You may grade yourself as you rate your day. This is between you and God.

❑ Praise, worship, and thanksgiving   ❑ Family time

❑ Prayer and extraordinary prayer   ❑ Time with friends

❑ Reading and meditating on the Word of God   ❑ Reaching the lost

❑ Fasting and other sacrifices   ❑ Eating right and exercising

❑ Serving others in Christ-like love   ❑ Organizing myself to serve God

"I am losing all hope; I am paralyzed with fear. I remember the days of old. I ponder all your great works. I think about what you have done" (Psalm 143:4-5).

Only 23 days to go in your *Countdown to Hope.*

RELEASING HOPE BY FORGIVENESS

"If you forgive those who sin against you, your heavenly
Father will forgive you. But if you refuse to forgive others, your
Father will not forgive your sins" (Matthew 6:14-15).

Some people have the same mentality as Jeremiah when he said, "I will never forget this awful time" (Lamentations 3:20). They have made up their minds not to forget terrible experiences or the wrongs that people have done to them, not realizing that unforgiveness hinders them from having hope and experiencing love. Forgiveness releases hope. Mercy toward others releases God's mercy toward you. God is merciful toward those whom He sees showing mercy to others (2 Samuel 22:26).

If you don't have people in your life who love you, maybe you carry a spirit of hatred. It didn't come from God. Maybe it didn't even come from your emotions at that moment. It may not be your hatred at all. Somebody did you wrong and you not only kept the incident in your mind but also allowed that person's spirit of hatred to come into you. You opened yourself up to a foreign body. You didn't protect yourself with hope and you didn't forgive that person with mercy.

Light dominates darkness unless you choose to allow darkness to dominate light in your life by remembering sad and bitter things. People say, "I can remember it just like it happened yesterday." They love talking about it. If you ask them for a testimony of something good that God did they can hardly think of anything. Divorced couples think about some wrong by the other person and refuse to think about all the good things they did together for the 20 or 30 years they were married. They don't remember the good with the same tenacity that they remember the evil.

Nobody has been mistreated as much as God, yet He still remains merciful. As Jeremiah was searching for hope, he recognized that great character quality of God and said, "His mercies are new every morning." When you change the judgment seat of your heart into a mercy seat, a door of hope can open and a stream of light can come in.

The most enduring things in your life should not be things that people did or didn't do for you. You can't take that to heaven. In fact, that attitude might keep you out.

Faith, hope, and love are enduring qualities. You should never lose hope. Open the door to hope by forgiveness and mercy. No matter how you feel about your shortcomings and your past failures at forgiveness, live in hope that your latter days will be great.

THROUGH-THE-BIBLE IN ONE YEAR DAILY READING GUIDE

Fill in the four Bible chapters for today's date from the guide in the back of this journal.

Today's Four Bible Readings	My Personal Notes
❏ _____	_____
❏ _____	_____
❏ _____	_____
❏ _____	_____

MY PRAYER PRIORITIES FOR TODAY

My Right Relationship With God

_____

_____

_____

_____

Leaders—Local, State, Nation, World

_____

_____

_____

_____

Needs of Family and Friends

_____

_____

_____

_____

Worldwide Revivals and Awakenings

_____

_____

_____

_____

Five-Fold Ministry Church Leadership

_____

_____

_____

_____

Praise and Thanksgiving

_____

_____

_____

_____

FORGIVENESS IS AN ACT OF THE WILL

"Forgiveness is an act of the will, and the will can function regardless of the temperature of the heart."—Corrie ten Boom (1892-1983)

MONEY MANAGEMENT AND WEALTH

_____
_____
_____
_____

_____
_____
_____
_____

"He does not retain His anger forever,
Because He delights in mercy.
He will again have compassion on us,
And will subdue our iniquities.
You will cast all our sins
Into the depths of the sea"
(Micah 7:18-19 NKJV).

MY TREASURE CHEST OF HOPE

Counting My Many Blessings

Planning My Hopes and Dreams

_____
_____
_____
_____
_____
_____
_____

_____
_____
_____
_____
_____
_____
_____

GREAT TESTIMONIES OF HOPE—CORRIE TEN BOOM

Forgiveness brings release to experience God's love

Corrie ten Boom (1892-1983) and her sister Betsie operated a watchmaker's shop with their father during the Nazi occupation of the Netherlands, but they also conducted a secret venture. As a devout Christian family, they protected Jews from their Nazi persecutors.

By the time they were arrested and taken away to concentration camps in February 1944, they had assisted in the escape of 800 Jews. Corrie's 1971 autobiography, *The Hiding Place*, written with John and Elizabeth Sherrill, and the film by the same name by Worldwide Pictures

(Billy Graham Evangelistic Association) documented their daring escapades and revealed the secret compartment where they hid their guests. Through an informer, the Gestapo discovered the ten Booms' underground work and arrested the ten Boom family and took them away. However, as the police entered Betsie was able to press an alarm bell and all the Jewish guests ran upstairs into the hiding place and later escaped.

Corrie's father Casper, 84, lived only ten days after the arrest. Her sister Betsie died at Ravensbruck, the notorious concentration camp. A nephew, Kik, died from abuse and starvation in another camp. However, through a clerical error Corrie was released from Ravensbruck and later traveled worldwide to tell people about the miracles of God's deliverance.

At the end of one of her talks, Corrie recognized a former guard from Ravensbruck in the audience. She had been teaching the Gospel of forgiveness in Jesus Christ, but here in front of her was someone who had been the epitome of evil. She remembered his cruelty to her and her sister Betsie and the leather crop that always swung from his belt.

As this man reached out his hand to Corrie after her message, he quoted from one of her favorite Scriptures that she used in her messages that "all our sins" are in "the depths of the sea" (Micah7:19, quoted on the previous page). She could sense that he did not remember her. He told her that he had become a Christian since Ravensbruck and he knew that God had forgiven him, but he asked her to forgive him, too.

For a few seconds she froze. Terrible memories flooded her mind. She said afterwards, "I wrestled with the most difficult thing I had ever had to do. For I had to do it—I knew that. The message that God forgives has a prior condition: that we forgive those who have injured us."

Corrie had established a home for victims of Nazi brutality in Holland, and she had discovered that only those who were able to forgive their enemies were able to return to a normal life. The others remained captive to their bitterness and lack of hope.

With great effort she reached out and shook his hand. At once she felt healing warmth come over her and a flood of God's love overwhelmed her. She said to him, "I forgive you, brother, with all my heart!"

Corrie traveled widely for many years until ill health finally forced her to give up her mission. She carried the Gospel to many nations and documented her travels in her book *Tramp for the Lord*.

In December 1967 she was honored as one of the Righteous Among the Nations by the State of Israel—non-Jews who risked their lives during the Holocaust to save Jews from extermination by the Nazis.

Do you pray for the Jews, the nation of Israel, and their enemies? Would you give your life so that other people could be saved and live?

24-HOUR PERSONAL ACCOUNTABILITY JOURNAL
How I spent every hour of my life today

12 AM	
1 AM	
2 AM	
3 AM	
4 AM	
5 AM	
6 AM	
7 AM	
8 AM	
9 AM	
10 AM	
11 AM	
12 PM	
1 PM	
2 PM	
3 PM	
4 PM	
5 PM	
6 PM	
7 PM	
8 PM	
9 PM	
10 PM	
11 PM	

TODAY'S JOURNAL OF PERSONAL INSIGHTS

_____

_____

_____

_____

_____

_____

_____

_____

_____

_____

"I will stand my watch
And set myself on the rampart,
And watch to see what He will say to me,
And what I will answer when I am corrected"
(Habakkuk 2:1 NKJV).

MY SELF-EVALUATION—HOW WELL DID I DO TODAY?

You may grade yourself as you rate your day. This is between you and God.

❑ Praise, worship, and thanksgiving   ❑ Family time

❑ Prayer and extraordinary prayer   ❑ Time with friends

❑ Reading and meditating on the Word of God ❑ Reaching the lost

❑ Fasting and other sacrifices   ❑ Eating right and exercising

❑ Serving others in Christ-like love   ❑ Organizing myself to serve God

"Look! A messenger is coming over the mountains with good news! He is bringing
a message of peace. Celebrate your festivals . . . and fulfill all your vows, for your
enemies from Nineveh will never invade your land again" (Nahum 1:15).

Only 22 days to go in your *Countdown to Hope.*

RESTORING HOPE BY REPENTANCE

David said, "You will show me the path of life;
In Your presence is fullness of joy;
At Your right hand are pleasures forevermore"
(Psalm 16:11 NKJV).

W hen you sin against God and repent with sincere sorrow for your sin, hope is restored and you receive assurance that you are forgiven. That gives you reason to rejoice. David was a sinner but he said, "You will show me the path of life; In Your presence is fullness of joy; At Your right hand are pleasures forevermore" (Psalm 16:11 NKJV).

When Peter preached from that messianic passage in Psalms after the outpouring of the Holy Spirit, thousands were saved. He said:

"Therefore did my heart rejoice, and my tongue was
glad; moreover also my flesh shall rest in hope: Because
thou wilt not leave my soul in hell" (Acts 2:26-27 KJV).

Jesus was literally dying and going to hell in our place, but God would not leave Him in hell and He will not leave you in hell. Hell is not your ordained place. No matter what you are going through or how things look now, rest in hope and then God will give you reason to rejoice. It will all work out. Live by the hope that God will surely come through for you. Experience the assurance that comes from knowing that you are on the Lord's side. Your calling is so much higher than your experiences.

Paul said, "For God, who commanded the light to shine out of darkness, hath shined in our hearts, to give the light of the knowledge of the glory of God in the face of Jesus Christ" (2 Corinthians 4:6 KJV).

He wrote, "We are pressed on every side by troubles, but we are not crushed and broken. We are perplexed, but we don't give up and quit. We are hunted down, but God never abandons us. We get knocked down, but we get up again and keep going" (2 Corinthians 4:8-9).

That is because when you become born again, the light of hope comes on inside of you. That light illuminates your understanding. You can see things "in a new light."

The only true light that unsaved people will ever see has to come through you. You are an ambassador in the earth carrying Jesus, the hope of the world. Regardless of how much education or wealth they have, they cannot receive the light until you give it to them. Have you repented and received assurance of His forgiveness? Will you take that light to others?

THROUGH-THE-BIBLE IN ONE YEAR DAILY READING GUIDE

Fill in the four Bible chapters for today's date from the guide in the back of this journal.

Today's Four Bible Readings	My Personal Notes
❏ _____	_____
❏ _____	_____
❏ _____	_____
❏ _____	_____

MY PRAYER PRIORITIES FOR TODAY

My Right Relationship With God

_____
_____
_____
_____

Leaders—Local, State, Nation, World

_____
_____
_____
_____

Needs of Family and Friends

_____
_____
_____
_____

Worldwide Revivals and Awakenings

_____
_____
_____
_____

Five-Fold Ministry Church Leadership

_____
_____
_____
_____

Praise and Thanksgiving

_____
_____
_____
_____

LOVE HEALS A WOUNDED HEART

"My heart that wounded was before,
Kindly he bound, therein did he pour
Love's healing quintessence."
—James McGready (1763-1817)

MONEY MANAGEMENT AND WEALTH

_____   _____
_____   _____
_____   _____
_____   _____
_____   _____

*"So he took me in the Spirit to a great, high mountain, and he showed me the holy
city, Jerusalem, descending out of heaven from God. It shone with the glory of God
and sparkled like a precious stone—like jasper as clear as crystal"
(Revelation 21:10-11).*

MY TREASURE CHEST OF HOPE

Counting My Many Blessings   Planning My Hopes and Dreams

_____   _____
_____   _____
_____   _____
_____   _____
_____   _____
_____   _____
_____   _____
_____   _____

GREAT TESTIMONIES OF HOPE—FRONTIER CAMP MEETINGS

Lawlessness never returned after ministers brought people to repentance

After the conclusion of the American Revolution, churches
declined in spiritual fervor and frontier areas like Kentucky became pagan
and populated by unrepentant criminals.

Ministers began praying for a new spiritual awakening and their
concerns brought them together even though they represented different
denominations. Many were circuit riders on the move from place to place,
overseeing two or three or more churches single-handedly. They humbled
themselves before God and one another and admitted they needed a
supernatural breakthrough in their midst.

In 1796, a praying Presbyterian named James McGready arrived
in Logan County, Kentucky, to pastor churches in Red River, Gasper
River, and Muddy River. Although the churches were small and the

Christians were outnumbered by the murderers, thieves, and other criminals, McGready's penetrating messages were fire and brimstone. Known as a "son of thunder," like James and John, Jesus' disciples, he preached so powerfully that another pastor said of him, "My mind was chained by him, and followed him closely in his rounds of heaven, earth, and hell with feelings indescribable." His Christ-like toughness tempered with humility was just what the rough frontier needed.

Rev. John Andrews, one of his contemporaries, recalled, "Although he did not fail to preach Jesus Christ . . . yet he was more distinguished by a talent for depicting the guilty and deplorable situation of impenitent sinners, and the awful consequences of their rebellion against God, without speedy repentance unto life and a living faith in the blood of sprinkling. . . . Some of the traits in Mr. M'Gready's character as a private Christian which are worthy of our imitation were his fervent piety, his unaffected humility, his earnest, persevering supplications at the Throne of Grace, his resignation to the will of God under the afflictions, bereavements and poverty, with which he was tried in this world."

In June 1800, McGready's Red River church sponsored a four-day Communion (conference where the focal point was the partaking of communion). Four or five hundred attended, including members of his other two churches and ministers from other denominations, who were also asked to preach.

On the final day, such a sudden move of God occurred that people began screaming for mercy and the floor was covered with those slain in the spirit. This had never happened there before.

McGready scheduled another communion for July in Gasper River. The word spread quickly and people came from as far as 100 miles away—a total of 8,000 flooding the roadways. Unusual physical manifestations occurred again and souls were saved.

In the summer of 1801, because of the excitement that had been building and the great amount of publicity, 25,000 people from many states and denominations came to Cane Ridge. Roads were clogged with people.

Over the next few years, the camp meetings continued to gain momentum, resulting in a spiritual awakening on the frontier. Camp meetings became so popular that in one year, 1811, it was estimated that one third of the entire American population attended at least one camp meeting. So many sinners came that watchmen with sticks patrolled the grounds each night to stop any sexual incidents and some states prohibited the sale of alcohol for miles around.

After the conversions and the strengthening of the churches, the Kentucky frontier never returned to its earlier state of lawlessness.

24-HOUR PERSONAL ACCOUNTABILITY JOURNAL
How I spent every hour of my life today

12 AM	
1 AM	
2 AM	
3 AM	
4 AM	
5 AM	
6 AM	
7 AM	
8 AM	
9 AM	
10 AM	
11 AM	
12 PM	
1 PM	
2 PM	
3 PM	
4 PM	
5 PM	
6 PM	
7 PM	
8 PM	
9 PM	
10 PM	
11 PM	

TODAY'S JOURNAL OF PERSONAL INSIGHTS

_____

_____

_____

_____

_____

_____

_____

_____

_____

_____

_____

"That is why you should examine yourself before eating the bread and drinking from the cup. For if you eat the bread or drink the cup unworthily, not honoring the body of Christ, you are eating and drinking God's judgment upon yourself"
(1 Corinthians 11:28-29).

MY SELF-EVALUATION—HOW WELL DID I DO TODAY?

You may grade yourself as you rate your day. This is between you and God.

❑ Praise, worship, and thanksgiving   ❑ Family time

❑ Prayer and extraordinary prayer   ❑ Time with friends

❑ Reading and meditating on the Word of God ❑ Reaching the lost

❑ Fasting and other sacrifices   ❑ Eating right and exercising

❑ Serving others in Christ-like love   ❑ Organizing myself to serve God

"Each of you must turn from your sins and turn to God, and be baptized in the name of Jesus Christ for the forgiveness of your sins. Then you will receive the gift of the Holy Spirit. This promise is to you and to your children, and even to the Gentiles—all who have been called by the Lord our God" (Acts 2:38-39).

Only 21 days to go in your *Countdown to Hope.*

INCREASING THE REACH OF YOUR PRAYERS BY HOPE

"The instant I speak concerning a nation and concerning a
kingdom, to pluck up, to pull down, and to destroy it,
if that nation against whom I have spoken turns from its evil,
I will relent of the disaster that I thought to bring upon it"
(Jeremiah 18:7-8 NKJV).

How many people of God in our day pray with such spiritual authority that national leaders are convicted of sin, repent, and are changed? John Knox did and Scotland and other nations were affected. When Christians are uncertain of their spiritual authority, they won't speak the Word of God to civil authorities. However, when they have the habit of self-judgment, they have confidence to hope in the power of their prayers.

Jesus said to judge yourself first, then speak to others.

> *"The standard you use in judging is the standard by which you will be judged. And why worry about a speck in your friend's eye when you have a log in your own? How can you think of saying to your friend, 'Let me help you get rid of that speck in your eye,' when you can't see past the log in your own eye? Hypocrite! First get rid of the log in your own eye; then you will see well enough to deal with the speck in your friend's eye" (Matthew 7:2-5).*

Sinners try to use Jesus' words to shut us down when we call out their sin to help them avert God's judgment, but Nineveh repented when Jonah called out the sins of those people. A society is sadly regressed when it doesn't have even that level of sensitivity to God's Word.

Some leaders in political parties today are like Pharaoh. They are hardened to the Word of God that could save them and the rest of the nation from God's wrath. Could God promote you to the position of confronting a leader—with respect and godly fear—and count on you to stand strong because you had received His instructions through prayer and a consecrated life? Do you believe in God's judgment on rulers enough to face them down as Moses did—for their sake and the sake of the nation— or do you allow people to shut down what God gives you in prayer?

Why should the ungodly rule? Why not Christians with character? I dare you to hope that your prayers and your boldness in confronting leaders could restore America to spiritual leadership of the world.

THROUGH-THE-BIBLE IN ONE YEAR DAILY READING GUIDE

Fill in the four Bible chapters for today's date from the guide in the back of this journal.

Today's Four Bible Readings	My Personal Notes
❑ _____	_____
❑ _____	_____
❑ _____	_____
❑ _____	_____

MY PRAYER PRIORITIES FOR TODAY

My Right Relationship With God

_____
_____
_____

Leaders—Local, State, Nation, World

_____
_____
_____

Needs of Family and Friends

_____
_____
_____

Worldwide Revivals and Awakenings

_____
_____
_____

Five-Fold Ministry Church Leadership

_____
_____
_____

Praise and Thanksgiving

_____
_____
_____

PRAYER FOR A NATION'S SINFUL LEADERS

". . . how fearful and terrible it is to fall into his hands without hope of mercy; and what is that his unspeakable mercy which yet again he offers unto you; and that it may please his eternal goodness to endue you with such wisdom, prudence, and fortitude, that seeing his good pleasure in his word revealed, without all fear you may follow the same." —John Knox (c. 1514-1572)

MONEY MANAGEMENT AND WEALTH

_____   _____
_____   _____
_____   _____
_____   _____

*"I urge you, first of all, to pray for all people. Ask God to help them; intercede on
their behalf, and give thanks for them. Pray this way for kings and all who are in
authority so that we can live peaceful and quiet lives marked by godliness and
dignity. This is good and pleases God our Savior, who wants everyone to be saved
and to understand the truth. For there is only one God and
one Mediator who can reconcile God and humanity—the man Christ Jesus.
He gave his life to purchase freedom for everyone" (1 Timothy 2:1-6).*

MY TREASURE CHEST OF HOPE

Counting My Many Blessings   Planning My Hopes and Dreams

_____   _____
_____   _____
_____   _____
_____   _____
_____   _____
_____   _____
_____   _____

GREAT TESTIMONIES OF HOPE—JOHN KNOX

Pastor with courage to pray for leaders and influence nations

Mary Queen of Scots reportedly said, "I fear the prayers of John
Knox more than all the assembled armies of Europe."
John Knox (c.1514-1572) greatly admired George Wishart, a
leader of the Scottish Reformation who was martyred for his faith in an age
of murder and intrigue in church and state issues that we can hardly
imagine today. The Scottish Protestants saw that Knox was extremely
gifted and pressured him to become a public preacher instead of a quiet
scholar, as he preferred.

From then on, Knox followed that calling. He became the leader of the Protestant Reformation in Scotland and his teachings greatly influenced the future of America's churches and civil government.

During his lifetime, many Christians and members of royalty were put to death. Knox managed to survive many close escapes, but Mary Queen of Scots, who feared his prayers, was eventually executed by her rival, Elizabeth I of England. Knox prayed for God's mercy on the nations' rulers for all of the killing and persecution, calling the rulers to repentance.

LIFE AND INFLUENCE OF JOHN KNOX (c.1514-1572)

- *Born in Scotland.* Follower of George Wishart, martyred in 1546. Knox was captured by the French and forced to serve as a galley slave until freed by the pro-Protestant English King Edward VI. Edward VI died in 1553.

- *Taught by John Calvin.* With the Catholic Queen Mary Tudor ("Bloody Mary") on the throne of England, and Mary Guise on the throne of Scotland, Knox fled to Geneva, Switzerland, joining others studying under John Calvin. There he embraced Calvin's teachings of the "reformed" movement and developed an English/Scottish work. He pastored an English church in Geneva and spread the movement to Scotland primarily through letters.

- *Returned to Scotland in 1559 as leader of Protestant rebellion* against the French-Catholic regent of Scotland, Mary of Guise, who died suddenly in 1560. Mary's daughter, Mary Queen of Scots, took the throne, but was unpopular. She fled to England, where Elizabeth I placed her under house arrest, then eventually had her executed.

- *Reshaped Church and society* along lines of Calvinism and his own biblical insights regarding governmental structure of the church.

- *Birthed "Presbyterian" or representative church government.* The people elected elders or "presbyters" in the church. Church leaders were not appointed by kings or other political rulers.

- *America's representative form of government* that was included in the U. S. Constitution (1789) and the constitutions of many states was inspired in part by Knox and Calvin.

24-HOUR PERSONAL ACCOUNTABILITY JOURNAL
How I spent every hour of my life today

12 AM	
1 AM	
2 AM	
3 AM	
4 AM	
5 AM	
6 AM	
7 AM	
8 AM	
9 AM	
10 AM	
11 AM	
12 PM	
1 PM	
2 PM	
3 PM	
4 PM	
5 PM	
6 PM	
7 PM	
8 PM	
9 PM	
10 PM	
11 PM	

Today's Journal of Personal Insights

_____

_____

_____

_____

_____

_____

_____

_____

_____

_____

_____

_____

" 'The Lord will judge his own people.' It is a terrible thing to fall into the hands of the living God. Don't ever forget those early days when you first learned about Christ. Remember how you remained faithful even though it meant terrible suffering" (Hebrews 10:30-32).

My Self-Evaluation—How Well Did I Do Today?

You may grade yourself as you rate your day. This is between you and God.

❑ Praise, worship, and thanksgiving   ❑ Family time

❑ Prayer and extraordinary prayer   ❑ Time with friends

❑ Reading and meditating on the Word of God   ❑ Reaching the lost

❑ Fasting and other sacrifices   ❑ Eating right and exercising

❑ Serving others in Christ-like love   ❑ Organizing myself to serve God

"If you make the LORD your refuge, if you make the Most High your shelter, no evil will conquer you; no plague will come near your dwelling" (Psalm 91:9-10).

Only 20 days to go in your _Countdown to Hope._

HOPE FOR FINANCIAL INDEPENDENCE

"And of the children of Issachar, which were men that had
understanding of the times, to know what Israel ought to do"
(1 Chronicles 12:32 KJV).

Jesus' resurrection was the beginning of a new financial era for Christians, so why are so many Christians broke? How can we become better at understanding the times and regain our hope of prosperity and financial independence?

The Puritans understood the application of the Bible to financial systems when they developed American capitalism. However, capitalism without Christ as the foundation results in greed and pride. Without a redemptive understanding of the purpose of money, people make money and take the glory for it themselves instead of giving the glory to God.

Jesus told the Church to make disciples of nations, but instead of leading in every natural realm and creating wealth to establish His kingdom in the earth (Deuteronomy 8:18), the Church has developed a survivalist mentality. We are whipped and functioning under the heel of leaders when we are supposed to be discipling nations with the Gospel.

Christians have been spiritually astute but naturally ignorant. If you don't understand the times, as the sons of Issachar did, you will become a slave of the times. Most people go to church to be inspired but not to find practical ways to get wealth. They have spiritual vision but not natural application. It is time for Christians to stop being slaves to debt and start using their spiritual inspiration to get financial insight and wealth.

Christians represent Christ. You are a leader who needs financial resources to lead others. When you expect to increase financially, you don't oversleep as an employee because you are preparing to own the company. You make an effort to get to work on time. You submit to accountability. You practice forecasting and projecting. You never say, "This is too difficult for me," because you know that God has a solution.

David brought together prophetically Jesus' three ministries as prophet, priest, and king. Under Jesus' last ministry as King, Christians move outside of the church buildings to once again dominate in the government and the marketplace, because Jesus said we must rule in every area of life. Now is the time to hope and prepare for prosperity.

Take time to write the vision God gives you, as Habakkuk did. Restore your hope that you can prosper and be financially independent regardless of the economy—because God is with you.

THROUGH-THE-BIBLE IN ONE YEAR DAILY READING GUIDE

Fill in the four Bible chapters for today's date from the guide in the back of this journal.

Today's Four Bible Readings	My Personal Notes
❑ _____	_____
❑ _____	_____
❑ _____	_____
❑ _____	_____

MY PRAYER PRIORITIES FOR TODAY

My Right Relationship With God

_____
_____
_____

Leaders—Local, State, Nation, World

_____
_____
_____

Needs of Family and Friends

_____
_____
_____

Worldwide Revivals and Awakenings

_____
_____
_____

Five-Fold Ministry Church Leadership

_____
_____
_____

Praise and Thanksgiving

_____
_____
_____

CARRY ON A PLAN FOR YOUR PROSPERITY

"Have hope, have faith, have courage, and carry on."—Maggie Walker (1867-1934)

Money Management and Wealth

_____   _____
_____   _____
_____   _____
_____   _____

"Always remember that it is the LORD your God who gives you power to become
rich, and he does it to fulfill the covenant he made with your ancestors"
(Deuteronomy 8:18).

My Treasure Chest of Hope

Counting My Many Blessings   Planning My Hopes and Dreams
_____   _____
_____   _____
_____   _____
_____   _____
_____   _____
_____   _____
_____   _____
_____   _____

Great Testimonies of Hope—Maggie Walker

Daughter of slaves becomes first woman to charter a U. S. bank

In 1903 a Black woman who was the daughter of slaves founded the St. Luke Penny Savings Bank in the former capital of the Confederacy—Richmond, Virginia. Maggie Walker (1867-1934) also served as the bank's first president, which gave her the status of the first woman to charter a bank in the United States. When the bank merged with two other Richmond banks to become the Consolidated Bank and Trust Company, she became chairman of the board of directors. The bank she founded more than a century ago is still in existence in Richmond. It is the oldest bank continually operated by Black Americans in the United States.

Maggie's vision for financial success came from her faith in Jesus Christ and her commitment to church life. When Blacks came out of slavery and formed communities, the first thing they did was establish a church. The pastor was a leader in the community. Within the church, pastors and leaders created self-help societies and businesses to provide burial insurance and other services for their people that the White community would not properly provide.

When Maggie was 14 years old, she joined the local council of the Independent Order of St. Luke. It had been established by church people to care for the sick and aged and to assure that Black people received a proper burial. It also encouraged self-help and godly character. She became an elected delegate two years later and was an elected officer by age 17. Her financial insight and strong policy structures helped the organization to emerge from its former difficulties and thrive.

The St. Luke Penny Savings Bank gave Black Americans with few financial resources the hope that even children who saved as much as a penny regularly could build a savings account and eventually become prosperous. She also created hope for financial prosperity by opening a department store where Black women could work as clerks and earn as much as White women.

The goal of the St. Luke Penny Savings Bank was not only to encourage savings but also to help Black citizens to purchase their own homes through bank loans. By 1920, the bank had assisted with the purchase of approximately 600 homes in spite of the environment of prejudice and oppression. By 1924, the Independent Order of St. Luke had assets of almost $400,000.

Maggie's parents, Elizabeth and William Mitchell, were slaves in the Richmond mansion of Elizabeth Van Lew, who was secretly an abolitionist and Northern spy. A few years after the Civil War, the Mitchells moved into a small house. Maggie's father died tragically and her mother supported the family by doing laundry. Ironically, Maggie's husband would also die under tragic circumstances when he was shot by their son in what the court ruled as an accidental shooting. Her son was so devastated by the ordeal that he died a few years later.

Maggie never gave up her goals in spite of family tragedies and personal ill health. She spent her latter years in a wheelchair because of injuries from a fall and diabetes, which would eventually cause her death.

Maintaining hope in the midst of challenges is the heritage of every Christian. Achieving financial success should also be our hope.

Maggie Walker's home is now a National Historic Site in Richmond. It stands as a witness to what hope can do.

24-HOUR PERSONAL ACCOUNTABILITY JOURNAL
How I spent every hour of my life today

12 AM	
1 AM	
2 AM	
3 AM	
4 AM	
5 AM	
6 AM	
7 AM	
8 AM	
9 AM	
10 AM	
11 AM	
12 PM	
1 PM	
2 PM	
3 PM	
4 PM	
5 PM	
6 PM	
7 PM	
8 PM	
9 PM	
10 PM	
11 PM	

TODAY'S JOURNAL OF PERSONAL INSIGHTS

_____

_____

_____

_____

_____

_____

_____

_____

_____

_____

"I will stand upon my watch, and set me upon the tower, and will watch to see what he will say unto me, and what I shall answer when I am reproved. And the LORD answered me, and said, Write the vision, and make it plain upon tables, that he may run that readeth it. For the vision is yet for an appointed time, but at the end it shall speak, and not lie: though it tarry, wait for it; because it will surely come, it will not tarry" (Habakkuk 2:1-3 KJV).

MY SELF-EVALUATION—HOW WELL DID I DO TODAY?

You may grade yourself as you rate your day. This is between you and God.

❑ Praise, worship, and thanksgiving   ❑ Family time

❑ Prayer and extraordinary prayer   ❑ Time with friends

❑ Reading and meditating on the Word of God ❑ Reaching the lost

❑ Fasting and other sacrifices   ❑ Eating right and exercising

❑ Serving others in Christ-like love   ❑ Organizing myself to serve God

"I assure you, those who listen to my message and believe in God who sent me have eternal life. They will never be condemned for their sins, but they have already passed from death into life" (John 5:24).

Only 19 days to go in your *Countdown to Hope.*

DECIDING TO HAVE HOPE FOR OTHERS

*"Everything I had hoped for from the LORD is lost! The thought
of my suffering and homelessness is bitter beyond words. I will
never forget this awful time, as I grieve over my loss.
Yet I still dare to hope" (Lamentations 3:18-21).*

When everything the prophet Jeremiah had hoped for seemed lost, he still made a decision to hope. Because Jeremiah decided to hope and he prayed and preached about his hope, God revealed the light of His goodness to the nation of Israel in spite of the darkness of that day.

When you make a decision to hope, that decision affects your life and it also helps others. When you refuse to give in to the pressures of despair, you can challenge every negative word and resist every work of darkness that does not conform to God's reality because you know that some day every knee will bow and every tongue will confess that Jesus Christ is Lord (Philippians 2:10-11). Bow to Him now and confess that He is Lord over every circumstance and the only hope for the world.

God will have His way in the world, and He wants you to see it the way He sees it. You will yield to the reality of His power on the earth either by revelation or by tribulation. When you decide by revelation that He is Lord, you release yourself to hope. That is what happened to Jeremiah. He remembered what he knew about God and he had hope.

When Jesus says, "You are the light of the world," He expects you to keep your light shining in the darkness for the sake of others. When you walk as the light of the world, your hope illumines the path ahead. When you never compromise or abdicate from God's standards, those standards give others light to live by.

In the great spiritual revivals and awakenings of history, someone refused to yield to any other reality than the reality of God in the midst of everything. When you give God glory in the midst of trials, hope comes alive. You become someone to follow. Even when others are overtaken by experiences, you are not. Your God is unchanging even in changing times. He says, "I am the LORD, and I do not change" (Malachi 3:6).

Jeremiah declared his negatives first. Sometimes it is good to get that out, but then he declared the bottom line. "Yet I still dare to hope."

Through-the-Bible in One Year Daily Reading Guide

Fill in the four Bible chapters for today's date from the guide in the back of this journal.

Today's Four Bible Readings	My Personal Notes
☐ _____	_____
☐ _____	_____
☐ _____	_____
☐ _____	_____

My Prayer Priorities for Today

My Right Relationship With God

_____
_____
_____

Leaders—Local, State, Nation, World

_____
_____
_____

Needs of Family and Friends

_____
_____
_____

Worldwide Revivals and Awakenings

_____
_____
_____

Five-Fold Ministry Church Leadership

_____
_____
_____

Praise and Thanksgiving

_____
_____
_____

Ignore the Clouds and Seek God

"Both you and I want a deeper awakening, which will produce a death to outward things and speculative knowledge. Let us shut our eyes to the gilded clouds without us; let us draw inward, and search after God, if haply we may find him. Let us hold our confidence, though we are often constrained against hope to believe in hope."—John Wesley (1703-1791)

MONEY MANAGEMENT AND WEALTH

_____   _____
_____   _____
_____   _____
_____   _____
_____   _____

"That they should seek the Lord, if haply they might feel after him, and find him, though he be not far from every one of us" (Acts 17:27 KJV).

MY TREASURE CHEST OF HOPE

Counting My Many Blessings   Planning My Hopes and Dreams

_____   _____
_____   _____
_____   _____
_____   _____
_____   _____
_____   _____
_____   _____
_____   _____
_____   _____

GREAT TESTIMONIES OF HOPE—MORAVIANS AND WESLEY

Seeing the courage of Christians in a storm changed the life of a leader

The following excerpt from the journal of John Wesley (1703-1791) is his honest account of an incident that occurred during his journey by ship from England to the colony of Georgia in 1736. He describes how the "Germans"—the Moravian Christians onboard—through their servitude and their courage during a storm at sea, gave such a testimony of hope that he recognized that he did not know Jesus as they did. This eventually resulted in his being born again and then leading one of the greatest spiritual awakenings in history, including the birth of the Methodist Church.

"Sunday, [January] 25 [1736].—At noon our third storm began. At four it was more violent than before. At seven I went to the Germans. I had long before observed the great seriousness of

*their behavior. Of their humility they had given a continual proof
by performing those servile offices for the other passengers,
which none of the English would undertake; for which they
desired and would receive no pay, saying, 'it was good for their
proud hearts,' and 'their loving Saviour had done more for them.'
And every day had given them an occasion of showing a meekness
which no injury could move. If they were pushed, struck, or
thrown down, they rose again and went away; but no complaint
was found in their mouth. There was now an opportunity of trying
whether they were delivered from the spirit of fear, as well as
from that of pride, anger and revenge.*

*"In the midst of the psalm . . . the sea broke over, split the
mainsail in pieces, covered the ship, and poured in between the
decks, as if the great deep had already swallowed us up. A
terrible screaming began among the English. The Germans
calmly sang on. I asked one of them afterward, 'Were you not
afraid?' He answered, 'I thank God, no.' I asked, 'But were not
your women and children afraid?' He replied, mildly, 'No; our
women and children are not afraid to die.' . . .*

"Saturday, [February] 7 [After safely landing in Georgia.]

*"Mr. Oglethorpe returned from Savannah with Mr. Spangenberg,
one of the pastors of the Germans. I soon found what spirit he was
of and asked his advice with regard to my own conduct. He said,
'My brother, I must first ask you one or two questions. Have you
the witness within yourself? Does the Spirit of God bear witness
with your spirit that you are a child of God?' I was surprised, and
knew not what to answer. He observed it and asked, 'Do you
know Jesus Christ?' I paused and said, 'I know He is the Saviour
of the world.' 'True,' replied he; 'but do you know He has saved
you?' I answered, 'I hope He has died to save me.' He only
added, 'Do you know yourself?' I said, 'I do.' But I fear they were
vain words."*

At the time of Wesley's journey, he was a missionary and had
been leading others in a sacrificial lifestyle of following the Bible in a
group called the Holy Club at Oxford University. However, when Wesley
saw the Moravians' dependence on God, he admitted he was not truly
saved. It was an important turning point in his walk of faith and in his
desire to know God. After he turned around, he led a spiritual awakening
that nearly three centuries later is still affecting nations.

24-HOUR PERSONAL ACCOUNTABILITY JOURNAL
How I spent every hour of my life today

12 AM	
1 AM	
2 AM	
3 AM	
4 AM	
5 AM	
6 AM	
7 AM	
8 AM	
9 AM	
10 AM	
11 AM	
12 PM	
1 PM	
2 PM	
3 PM	
4 PM	
5 PM	
6 PM	
7 PM	
8 PM	
9 PM	
10 PM	
11 PM	

TODAY'S JOURNAL OF PERSONAL INSIGHTS

_____

_____

_____

_____

_____

_____

_____

_____

_____

_____

_____

_____

_____

_____

"Do not be like a senseless horse or mule that needs a bit and bridle to keep it under control. Many sorrows come to the wicked, but unfailing love surrounds those who trust the LORD" (Psalm 32:9-10).

MY SELF-EVALUATION—HOW WELL DID I DO TODAY?

You may grade yourself as you rate your day. This is between you and God.

❑ Praise, worship, and thanksgiving ❑ Family time

❑ Prayer and extraordinary prayer ❑ Time with friends

❑ Reading and meditating on the Word of God ❑ Reaching the lost

❑ Fasting and other sacrifices ❑ Eating right and exercising

❑ Serving others in Christ-like love ❑ Organizing myself to serve God

"Whom have I in heaven but you? I desire you more than anything on earth. My health may fail, and my spirit may grow weak, but God remains the strength of my heart; he is mine forever" (Psalm 73:25-26).

Only 18 days to go in your *Countdown to Hope.*

Uniting Families Through Hope

"For this is the secret: Christ lives in you, and this is your
assurance that you will share in his glory. So everywhere we
go, we tell everyone about Christ. We warn them and teach
them with all the wisdom God has given us, for we want to
present them to God, perfect in their relationship to Christ"
(Colossians 1:27-28).

Every family needs a common hope or vision that all members of the family understand and keep before them. It may be represented by a family crest or coat of arms or something else that has meaning to your family—symbols that speak about who you are, where you have come from, and where you are going in Christ.

Christian families not only set a standard in their homes but also present a standard to the world. When your light grows dim and you are ashamed of who you are, you won't have the courage to defend the values that made your country great. However, when your family members support and encourage one another in the faith, their light shines brightly.

When church attendance becomes less important to the culture than a football game, hope can come alive through families who carry a common vision of Christ-likeness. Fathers take the lead by giving identity and value to their children. They set an example for the community of a family united by hope.

Some of the best Christian fathers in American history have been Black. During slavery, Black fathers valued their children so much that they were willing to risk their lives to protect them. Some escaped through the Underground Railroad so that they and their families could be free. After the Civil War released them from bondage, Black fathers would walk hundreds of miles searching for their lost wives and children.

According to Malachi 4, a fatherless generation is a cursed generation. Today, lack of hope has caused many fathers of all races to no longer see themselves with the kind of God-centered, generational vision that fathers had in the past. They need to be restored to the hope that the lives of their wives and children are important. They are made in God's image and have come together as a family in Christ to do His will. They are people of value whom God created for greatness as they follow Christ.

When fathers come to Christ and recapture faith and hope, they will take their families on an adventure with God. They will develop a unified family vision for transforming their homes and all the earth into the kingdom of God—in earth as it is in heaven.

THROUGH-THE-BIBLE IN ONE YEAR DAILY READING GUIDE

Fill in the four Bible chapters for today's date from the guide in the back of this journal.

Today's Four Bible Readings	My Personal Notes
❑ _____	_____
❑ _____	_____
❑ _____	_____
❑ _____	_____

MY PRAYER PRIORITIES FOR TODAY

My Right Relationship With God

_____
_____
_____
_____

Leaders—Local, State, Nation, World

_____
_____
_____
_____

Needs of Family and Friends

_____
_____
_____
_____

Worldwide Revivals and Awakenings

_____
_____
_____
_____

Five-Fold Ministry Church Leadership

_____
_____
_____
_____

Praise and Thanksgiving

_____
_____
_____
_____

CALLING MEN TO ARISE AND MAKE A DIFFERENCE

"The day dawns; the morning star is bright upon the horizon! . . . The chance is now given you to end in a day the bondage of centuries, and to rise in one bound from social degradation to the place of common equality with all other varieties of men." —Frederick Douglass (1817?-1895), calling men of color to fight in the Civil War

Money Management and Wealth

_____   _____
_____   _____
_____   _____
_____   _____
_____   _____

"Lord, you know the hopes of the helpless.
Surely you will hear their cries and comfort them" (Psalm 10:17).

My Treasure Chest of Hope

Counting My Many Blessings   Planning My Hopes and Dreams

_____   _____
_____   _____
_____   _____
_____   _____
_____   _____
_____   _____
_____   _____
_____   _____

Great Testimonies of Hope—Frederick Douglass

Father's hope for a different life for his children

Frederick Douglass (1817?-1895) was born a slave on the Eastern Shore of Maryland in about 1817. The actual year of his birth can only be approximated, since few accurate records were kept of slaves. From the time he was a child of six, Douglass had been determined to run away. His mother died when he was seven. When he was a teen, he brazenly took on his slave master in a physical fight that could have cost him his life. He defied the stereotype of an ignorant slave by first learning to read by bribing white boys and then studying in secret for years.

Ten years after escaping from the plantation and establishing himself as a free man in the North, Douglass had become an eloquent spokesman against the evils of slavery and a standard of reconciliation for both Black and White, Christian and non Christian. At that time, he wrote a letter to his former master in which he said he had no malice toward him but a sense of profound gratitude that as a father he could protect his children so they would never have to suffer such a fate as slavery. He described in his letter how slavery had attempted to destroy the Black family and his gratitude for his children's freedom:

> "So far as my domestic affairs are concerned, I can boast of as comfortable a dwelling as your own. I have an industrious and neat companion, and four dear children—the oldest a girl of nine years, and three fine boys, the oldest eight, the next six, and the youngest four years old. The three oldest are now going regularly to school—two can read and write, and the other can spell with tolerable correctness words of two syllables: Dear fellows! They are all in comfortable beds, and are sound asleep, perfectly secure under my own roof. There are no slave-holders here to rend my heart by snatching them from my arms, or blast a mother's dearest hopes by tearing them from her bosom.
>
> "These dear children are ours—not to work up into rice, sugar and tobacco, but to watch over, regard, and protect, and to rear them up in the nurture and admonition of the gospel—to train them up in the paths of wisdom and virtue, and, as far as we can to make them useful to the world and to themselves. Oh! sir, a slave holder never appears to me so completely an agent of hell, as when I think of and look upon my dear children. It is then that my feelings rise above my control. . . .
>
> "Your mind must have become darkened, your heart hardened, your conscience seared and petrified, or you would have long since thrown off the accursed load and sought relief at the hands of a sin-forgiving God."

We need to love our children more, the way Douglass loved his and as God loves us. We don't ever want them to think we don't believe in them or we don't have hope for their future and our future as a family. We need to see their potential and not their outward behavior, especially when their bad attitudes are directed toward us as their parents. That's when we need unconditional love to direct them to our Father. Black Americans of the past achieved victories against incredible odds. Their families were strong. They were great people of faith and financial provision.

We can restore the Black family, fix the broken educational system, and start businesses. We can develop the leadership potential of Black Americans to rebuild their communities, create wealth, and serve this nation as statesmen of character, helping to lead America to its rightful place in the world. By reaching out to Black Americans who have become "the least of these," the Church will receive the honor and praise of Christ.

24-HOUR PERSONAL ACCOUNTABILITY JOURNAL
How I spent every hour of my life today

12 AM	
1 AM	
2 AM	
3 AM	
4 AM	
5 AM	
6 AM	
7 AM	
8 AM	
9 AM	
10 AM	
11 AM	
12 PM	
1 PM	
2 PM	
3 PM	
4 PM	
5 PM	
6 PM	
7 PM	
8 PM	
9 PM	
10 PM	
11 PM	

TODAY'S JOURNAL OF PERSONAL INSIGHTS

_____

_____

_____

_____

_____

_____

_____

_____

_____

_____

_____

_____

_____

_____

"And the LORD our God commanded us to obey all these laws and to fear him for our own prosperity and well-being, as is now the case. For we are righteous when we obey all the commands the LORD our God has given us"
(Deuteronomy 6:24-25).

MY SELF-EVALUATION—HOW WELL DID I DO TODAY?

You may grade yourself as you rate your day. This is between you and God.

❑ Praise, worship, and thanksgiving ❑ Family time

❑ Prayer and extraordinary prayer ❑ Time with friends

❑ Reading and meditating on the Word of God ❑ Reaching the lost

❑ Fasting and other sacrifices ❑ Eating right and exercising

❑ Serving others in Christ-like love ❑ Organizing myself to serve God

"Why am I discouraged? Why is my heart so sad? I will put my hope in God! I will praise him again—my Savior and my God!" (Psalm 43:5).

Only 17 days to go in your *Countdown to Hope.*

SACRIFICING IN HOPES OF OTHERS' CHANGE

"God forbid that I should sin against the
Lord in ceasing to pray for you"
(1 Samuel 12:23 KJV).

When Jeremiah cried to the Lord in Lamentations, he was a man who represented God crying over the condition of His people. Jeremiah had given his life for the cause of God to pray for them.

Samuel said something similar to the people of Israel when they were terrified about what God would do to them because they had sinned and demanded a king. He reminded them of their favor with God and said, "He made you a special nation for himself. . . . God forbid that I should sin against the Lord in ceasing to pray for you" (1 Samuel 12:23 KJV).

Samuel and Jeremiah laid aside their own goals and made God's goals their reason for living. When you dedicate your life to God in that way, then God Himself is invested in you. He will keep your hope alive as long as His purposes are being fulfilled through your life.

Jeremiah never saw one of his prayers come to pass. He was thrown down into a well with mud and dung. He was taken captive to Babylon. He was rejected by his own people and did not have a single friend. Although God did not seem to be coming through for him he said, "Yet I still dare to hope."

I don't know how much hope you have, but I believe by the end of this journal your hope will have increased because the people of God are the only ones who can have true hope. Everybody else is faking it. If you seek God and He initiates your goals, you will have hope that lasts.

Jeremiah dared to hope in the midst of apparent failure because He knew that God had given him the burden to prophesy over the people. Samuel was disappointed that the people wanted a king instead of him, but He knew that God wanted him to keep praying for them, even in their rebellion. Everything you try to accomplish for yourself can be gone in a moment. Everything you do for God will accomplish its result.

People who are called by God to reach a certain group of people in a church, a community, or a nation like Israel or America can get discouraged at times, but the goal of God is for you to stay full of hope.

Don't give up on the people. Dare to hope that God will save them if you will stay faithful to make the sacrifices necessary to pray and speak for God into their lives.

THROUGH-THE-BIBLE IN ONE YEAR DAILY READING GUIDE

Fill in the four Bible chapters for today's date from the guide in the back of this journal.

Today's Four Bible Readings	My Personal Notes
❑ _____	_____
❑ _____	_____
❑ _____	_____
❑ _____	_____

MY PRAYER PRIORITIES FOR TODAY

My Right Relationship With God

_____
_____
_____

Leaders—Local, State, Nation, World

_____
_____
_____

Needs of Family and Friends

_____
_____
_____

Worldwide Revivals and Awakenings

_____
_____
_____

Five-Fold Ministry Church Leadership

_____
_____
_____

Praise and Thanksgiving

_____
_____
_____

HOPING TO HAVE THE CHARACTER OF CHRIST

"It is most evident that you must have a deep sympathy with heaven, its society, and its employments;—else you cannot by any means have a Christian hope. The Christian hope, is the hope of being like Christ; and for this, you must understand his character—must see its excellence, and the possibility of being like him; this will impel you to labor to be transformed into his likeness."
—Charles Finney (1792-1875)

MONEY MANAGEMENT AND WEALTH

_____   _____
_____   _____
_____   _____
_____   _____

"You have shown me the way of life, and
you will give me wonderful joy in your presence" (Acts 2:28).

MY TREASURE CHEST OF HOPE

Counting My Many Blessings   Planning My Hopes and Dreams

_____   _____
_____   _____
_____   _____
_____   _____
_____   _____
_____   _____
_____   _____
_____   _____

GREAT TESTIMONIES OF HOPE—CHARLES FINNEY

Committed to reaching people for Christ, regardless of sacrifice

The future American revivalist Charles Finney (1792-1875) as a young man was such a skeptic concerning Christianity that his Presbyterian pastor doubted if he could ever be saved. However, God was at work. Finney said later, "A little consideration convinced me that I was by no means in a state of mind to go to heaven if I should die. It seemed to me that there must be something in religion that was of infinite importance; and it was soon settled with me, that if the soul was immortal I needed a great change in my inward state to be prepared for happiness in heaven."

Finney was studying the law by reading William Blackstone's *Commentaries on the Laws of England*, the custom in that day. He found so many references to the Bible that he bought one—his first. Suddenly, he saw that he was not in a right inner relationship with God. His heart was evil and filled with pride. Under deep conviction, he escaped from the law office to the woods, where God showed him his sins, and he "fastened upon [these convictions] with the grasp of a drowning man."

Once he was saved, Finney's first major meetings as an evangelist were held at Evans Mills, New York. Although people enjoyed his sermons, two or three weeks passed with no one moved to accept Christ as Savior. In fact, no one was even familiar with that experience. Listeners became so agitated that he was in danger of being mobbed. He wrote in his *Memoirs* that he realized the situation called for extraordinary measures.

> *"But for that evening and the next day they were full of wrath. Deacon McC and myself agreed upon the spot, to spend the next day in fasting and prayer separately in the morning, and together in the afternoon. I learned in the course of the day that the people were threatening me—to ride me on a rail, to tar and feather me, and to give me a 'walking paper,' as they said. Some of them cursed me; and said that I had put them under oath, and made them swear that they would not serve God; that I had drawn them into a solemn and public pledge to reject Christ and His Gospel. This was no more than I expected. In the afternoon Deacon McC and I went into a grove together, and spent the whole afternoon in prayer. Just at evening the Lord gave us great enlargement, and promise of victory. Both of us felt assured that we had prevailed with God; and that, that night, the power of God would be revealed among the people.*
>
> *"As the time came for meeting, we left the woods and went to the village. The people were already thronging to the place of worship; and those that had not already gone, seeing us go through the villages turned out of their stores and places of business, or threw down their ball clubs where they were playing upon the green, and packed the house to its utmost capacity. . . .*
>
> *"The Spirit of God came upon me with such power, that. it was like opening a battery upon them. For more than an hour, and perhaps for an hour and a half, the Word of God came through me to them in a manner that I could see was carrying all before it. It was a fire and a hammer breaking the rock; and as the sword that was piercing to the dividing asunder of soul and spirit. I saw that a general conviction was spreading over the whole congregation. Many of them could not hold up their heads."*

After that crusade, Finney went on to bring about the conversion of half a million people and change the course of American and world history through his influence on society, including the abolition of slavery.

24-HOUR PERSONAL ACCOUNTABILITY JOURNAL
How I spent every hour of my life today

12 AM	
1 AM	
2 AM	
3 AM	
4 AM	
5 AM	
6 AM	
7 AM	
8 AM	
9 AM	
10 AM	
11 AM	
12 PM	
1 PM	
2 PM	
3 PM	
4 PM	
5 PM	
6 PM	
7 PM	
8 PM	
9 PM	
10 PM	
11 PM	

TODAY'S JOURNAL OF PERSONAL INSIGHTS

_____

_____

_____

_____

_____

_____

_____

_____

_____

_____

_____

_____

_____

_____

_____

"Try to live in peace with everyone, and seek to live a clean and holy life, for those who are not holy will not see the Lord" (Hebrews 12:14-15).

MY SELF-EVALUATION—HOW WELL DID I DO TODAY?

You may grade yourself as you rate your day. This is between you and God.

❑ Praise, worship, and thanksgiving   ❑ Family time

❑ Prayer and extraordinary prayer   ❑ Time with friends

❑ Reading and meditating on the Word of God   ❑ Reaching the lost

❑ Fasting and other sacrifices   ❑ Eating right and exercising

❑ Serving others in Christ-like love   ❑ Organizing myself to serve God

"For the promise is unto you, and to your children, and to all that are afar off, even as many as the Lord our God shall call" (Acts 2:39 KJV).

Only 16 days to go in your *Countdown to Hope.*

HOPING YOUR DONATIONS MAKE A DIFFERENCE

*" 'There is still one thing you lack,' Jesus said. 'Sell all you
have and give the money to the poor, and you will have
treasure in heaven. Then come, follow me' " (Luke 18:22).*

God wants you to prosper. The poor need your prosperity. They don't
need you to be numbered with them because you have no more money
than they do. Have hope that you can have the resources to give to those in
need and your donations can make a difference in many lives.

Almost all Christian leaders involved in evangelical revivals of
the past believed that transforming lifestyles and changing the condition of
society were of nearly equal importance to preaching the Gospel. In most
cases, that takes financial resources. That is why churches and most
ministries take offerings—to finance the work of reaching people for
Christ. They need resources to meet both spiritual and natural needs.

Charity is the obligation of every Christian whom Jesus has called
to both love God and love his neighbor as himself. Benevolence is not only
done for its own sake. It is a means toward a higher end—reaching the lost
and winning them to Christ. If you are rich in prayer, rich in the Word, rich
in consecration, there is nothing wrong with also being rich in money.
Somebody is handling the resources of the world. Why not you?

> *"The LORD will give you an abundance of good things in
> the land he swore to give your ancestors—many
> children, numerous livestock, and abundant crops. The
> LORD will send rain at the proper time from his rich
> treasury in the heavens to bless all the work you do. You
> will lend to many nations, but you will never need to
> borrow from them. If you listen to these commands of the
> LORD your God and carefully obey them, the LORD will
> make you the head and not the tail, and you will always
> have the upper hand" (Deuteronomy 28:11-14).*

You can be a bank instead of going to a bank. You can be a lender
whom others come to, not a borrower begging for a loan. You can be
empowering businesses instead of looking for others to empower you. If
your pastor wants a new building, you can be the first in line with a check.
You just have to keep your heart right. If the love of money does not
dominate your life but the love of God's wisdom and the fear of the Lord,
you can be trusted with handling money.

THROUGH-THE-BIBLE IN ONE YEAR DAILY READING GUIDE
Fill in the four Bible chapters for today's date from the guide in the back of this journal.

Today's Four Bible Readings	My Personal Notes
❑ _____	_____
❑ _____	_____
❑ _____	_____
❑ _____	_____

MY PRAYER PRIORITIES FOR TODAY

My Right Relationship With God	Leaders—Local, State, Nation, World
_____	_____
_____	_____
_____	_____

Needs of Family and Friends	Worldwide Revivals and Awakenings
_____	_____
_____	_____
_____	_____

Five-Fold Ministry Church Leadership	Praise and Thanksgiving
_____	_____
_____	_____
_____	_____

PERSEVERANCE TO GIVE IN SPITE OF THREATS
"We will persevere, come life or death."—Lewis Tappan (1788-1863).

Money Management and Wealth

_____   _____
_____   _____
_____   _____
_____   _____
_____   _____

"Beloved, I pray that you may prosper in all things and be in health,
just as your soul prospers" (3 John 2 NKJV).

My Treasure Chest of Hope

Counting My Many Blessings   Planning My Hopes and Dreams

_____   _____
_____   _____
_____   _____
_____   _____
_____   _____
_____   _____
_____   _____
_____   _____

Great Testimonies of Hope—Arthur and Lewis Tappan

Boldness to use their wealth for others

A few years ago a popular movie called *Amistad* directed by
Steven Spielberg told the story of slaves from West Africa who were
captured and sold illegally. They mutinied while onboard a slaving vessel
and commandeered the ship. Later they were captured in America, but their
cause was taken up by abolitionists who fought for their freedom.

The man chiefly responsible for funding their defense and
persuading the former President of the United States, John Quincy Adams,
to serve as their lawyer, was the wealthy Christian businessman Lewis
Tappan (1788-1863). He mobilized benefactors to finance the slaves'
defense and after the trial these benefactors formed the American
Missionary Association to continue the work.

In a wave of Christian unity birthed out of an early 19th-century
revival, Arthur and Lewis Tappan, their pastor, Charles Finney, and others
among the Presbyterians, Congregationalists, Methodists, Baptists and

Episcopalians sought to influence society in what Finney said was "being useful to the highest degree possible."

Finney said that anyone who claimed to be a Christian would of necessity be involved in the reform of society. Otherwise, they were backslidden. Christians working together for the reform of society through faith in Jesus Christ created major interdenominational movements like these in nineteenth-century America, forming a "Benevolent Empire."

CHRISTIAN ORGANIZATIONS IN THE 'BENEVOLENT EMPIRE'

- American Board of Commissioners for Foreign Missions (1810)
- American Education Society (1816)
- American Home Missionary Society (1826)
- American Bible Society (1816)
- American Tract Society (1826)
- American Sunday School Union (1817)
- American Temperance Society (1826)
- American Anti-Slavery Society (1833)
- American and Foreign Anti-Slavery Society (1840)
- American Missionary Association (1839)

As a Christian businessman, Lewis Tappan's life demonstrated biblical principles. He believed that God had given him his wealth and he should use it in a godly way. This included the principle of integrity, which led him to found a credit rating agency that became Dun and Bradstreet.

His faith also led him to give away such large sums of money that they actually influenced the course of American history in such moral causes as the abolition of slavery and education of the freed slaves, temperance, and honoring the Sabbath day. Their lives were threatened and their property destroyed. They were sometimes misunderstood. They were subject to the financial crises of the times and had to repay debtors and rebuild their finances after a major crash.

The Tappan brothers are rarely mentioned in history today, but their impact was noted in heaven. They remain an example of people who hope that their donations will make a difference that all of us can follow.

> *"Whatever measure you use in giving—large or small—*
> *it will be used to measure what is given back to you"*
> *(Luke 6:38).*

24-HOUR PERSONAL ACCOUNTABILITY JOURNAL
How I spent every hour of my life today

12 AM	
1 AM	
2 AM	
3 AM	
4 AM	
5 AM	
6 AM	
7 AM	
8 AM	
9 AM	
10 AM	
11 AM	
12 PM	
1 PM	
2 PM	
3 PM	
4 PM	
5 PM	
6 PM	
7 PM	
8 PM	
9 PM	
10 PM	
11 PM	

Today's Journal of Personal Insights

"Then at last everyone will say, 'There truly is a reward for those who live for God; surely there is a God who judges justly here on earth' " (Psalm 58:11).

My Self-Evaluation—How Well Did I Do Today?

You may grade yourself as you rate your day. This is between you and God.

❑ Praise, worship, and thanksgiving   ❑ Family time

❑ Prayer and extraordinary prayer   ❑ Time with friends

❑ Reading and meditating on the Word of God   ❑ Reaching the lost

❑ Fasting and other sacrifices   ❑ Eating right and exercising

❑ Serving others in Christ-like love   ❑ Organizing myself to serve God

"I pray that your hearts will be flooded with light so that you can understand the wonderful future he has promised to those he called. I want you to realize what a rich and glorious inheritance he has given to his people" (Ephesians 1:18).

Only 15 days to go in your *Countdown to Hope.*

SANCTIFYING YOURSELF TO SPREAD HOPE

*"And since we have a great High Priest who rules over God's
people, let us go right into the presence of God, with true
hearts fully trusting him. For our evil consciences have been
sprinkled with Christ's blood to make us clean, and our bodies
have been washed with pure water. Without wavering, let us
hold tightly to the hope we say we have, for God can be trusted
to keep his promise" (Hebrews 10:21-23).*

If somebody in the world could meet somebody like you, their whole
future would be changed. They not only need God. They need you,
because God is in you. You have the substance of heaven and you are in
there with God in prayer and fasting and have some consecration on you.
There is something about your life that helps people to be changed.

God chooses to give hope to the world by the hope that He gives
to you. If you lose your hope, the world's light starts to go out. If you lose
God's vision inside of you, the world is affected.

I have been in the Lord for 40 years but I still ask God to keep my
hope alive. I won't continue to live right just because I've been saved 40
years. I will live right with the daily help of God. My cleanliness is based
on my desire for God to keep me privately devout and secretly saved.

God wants your will. He wants you to live in such a way that
nobody has to watch over you and ask you accountability questions about
what you just did wrong because God is with you and His presence is
strong enough to keep you whole and clean.

If you do wrong, repent and do right. Ask God to give you the gift
of repentance. Through the blood of Jesus, all your sins will be forgiven.
The Bible says the blood of Jesus Christ, God's Son, cleanses you from all
unrighteousness (1 John 1:7). From that moment forward you can walk
with a divine sense of holiness. You can live a devout life.

Where you have been hopeless, ask God to help you to be
hopeful. Where you have given up, ask God to help you to stay in there,
and still dare to hope.

Jesus gave His life that you might have His life in you. When you
take communion, you partake of His body that was broken for you. You do
it in remembrance of Him. By faith you apply His body and blood to your
life and you are healed at both a personal and collective level. The body of
Christ is a clean, whole, healthy body because people like you are clean.

We are family. We are relatives. We have spots and wrinkles—
things we do by omission and things we do by commission—but we are
sanctified by the blood as we receive it in Jesus' name.

THROUGH-THE-BIBLE IN ONE YEAR DAILY READING GUIDE

Fill in the four Bible chapters for today's date from the guide in the back of this journal.

Today's Four Bible Readings	My Personal Notes
❏ _____	_____
❏ _____	_____
❏ _____	_____
❏ _____	_____

MY PRAYER PRIORITIES FOR TODAY

My Right Relationship With God

_____
_____
_____
_____

Leaders—Local, State, Nation, World

_____
_____
_____
_____

Needs of Family and Friends

_____
_____
_____
_____

Worldwide Revivals and Awakenings

_____
_____
_____
_____

Five-Fold Ministry Church Leadership

_____
_____
_____
_____

Praise and Thanksgiving

_____
_____
_____
_____

INNOCENT BLOOD CRIED FROM THE GROUND; SLAVERY ENDED

"The long night of affliction in the house of our bondage had passed, and that deeply desired and hoped for and prayed for time had come! The cries and groans and prayers of millions of poor and defenceless slaves, with the prayers of their friends in America, England, Ireland, Scotland, Wales, and everywhere, had reached the throne of God. Innocent blood of murdered men and women and children had cried unto God from the ground, and He in His own time, which is always the right time and best time, and in His own way, which is the very best way, answered that cry."—Thomas Lewis Johnson, former American slave (?1836-1921)

MONEY MANAGEMENT AND WEALTH

_____   _____
_____   _____
_____   _____
_____   _____

*"Think of ways to encourage one another to outbursts of love and good deeds.
And let us not neglect our meeting together, as some people do, but
encourage and warn each other, especially now that the
day of his coming back again is drawing near" (Hebrews 10:24-25).*

MY TREASURE CHEST OF HOPE

Counting My Many Blessings   Planning My Hopes and Dreams

_____   _____
_____   _____
_____   _____
_____   _____
_____   _____
_____   _____
_____   _____
_____   _____

GREAT TESTIMONIES OF HOPE—SLAVE COMES TO SALVATION

Desperate for God, a slave meets someone who shows him the way

In 1857, a slave named Thomas Lewis Johnson was in a state of
desperation, walking the streets of Richmond, Virginia. His despair was
deeper than his condition of slavery. He had a yearning inside for real
contact with God. He wrote of his anxiety in his autobiography *Twenty
Eight Years a Slave:*

> *"Matters came to such a pass that during the day I could scarcely
> speak to anyone; instead of being lively, and cheerful I was
> gloomy and nervous, and my master wanted to know what was
> wrong, and even threatened to send me to Georgia. But I had
> made up my mind that wherever I went I would not stop seeking
> religion until I found peace."*

As he was walking, he met another Black man who told him how to find Jesus. The words changed his life. He wrote:

> *"In the year 1857 there was a great revival in America. The coloured people thought the Judgment Day was coming. Everywhere we heard of great meetings and of thousands of souls being converted. In the Richmond tobacco factories, which employed many thousands of slaves, there were many converts daily. First one and then another of my friends would set out to 'seek religion.' . . .*
>
> *"One day I met a coloured man in the street, named Stephney Brown. He was a Christian, and quite an intelligent man. He explained to me the simple Gospel. He told me to go to God, and say:*
>
> *" 'Lord, have mercy upon me, a hell-deserving sinner, for Jesus' sake; set me out your way and not my way, for Jesus' sake.' . . .*
>
> *"As soon as my work was done for that night, and all was quiet, I resolved that, if I lived for a thousand years, I would never stop praying 'for Jesus' sake.' I went into the dining room, fell down upon my knees, and said: 'O Lord have mercy upon me, a hell-deserving sinner, for Jesus' sake.'*
>
> *"Then I became very happy. I got up and went into the porch. Everything appeared to be different to me. The very stars in the heaven seemed brighter, and I was feeling brighter and so very happy. I did not see any great sights, but there was an inward rejoicing. I had not done anything—I could not do anything—to merit this any more than the thief upon the cross, but my blessed Jesus had done it all; there was nothing for me to do."*

America had a spiritual awakening in those days, but it didn't end slavery. Not enough people realized that a judgment of God was coming because of this great national sin. People were getting saved but they did not apply their faith to corporate repentance on behalf of the nation, so God had to send a great Civil War less than four years later to free the slaves.

What we won't see by revelation, God must send by tribulation.

What new judgment is about to hit America? Will you consecrate yourself now so that you can hear His voice and repent for our nation?

24-HOUR PERSONAL ACCOUNTABILITY JOURNAL

How I spent every hour of my life today

12 AM	
1 AM	
2 AM	
3 AM	
4 AM	
5 AM	
6 AM	
7 AM	
8 AM	
9 AM	
10 AM	
11 AM	
12 PM	
1 PM	
2 PM	
3 PM	
4 PM	
5 PM	
6 PM	
7 PM	
8 PM	
9 PM	
10 PM	
11 PM	

TODAY'S JOURNAL OF PERSONAL INSIGHTS

_____

_____

_____

_____

_____

_____

_____

_____

_____

_____

_____

"Dear friends, if we deliberately continue sinning after we have received a full knowledge of the truth, there is no other sacrifice that will cover these sins. There will be nothing to look forward to but the terrible expectation of God's judgment" (Hebrews 10:26-27).

MY SELF-EVALUATION—HOW WELL DID I DO TODAY?

You may grade yourself as you rate your day. This is between you and God.

❑ Praise, worship, and thanksgiving ❑ Family time

❑ Prayer and extraordinary prayer ❑ Time with friends

❑ Reading and meditating on the Word of God ❑ Reaching the lost

❑ Fasting and other sacrifices ❑ Eating right and exercising

❑ Serving others in Christ-like love ❑ Organizing myself to serve God

"So be strong and take courage, all you who put your hope in the LORD!" (Psalm 31:24).

Only 14 days to go in your *Countdown to Hope.*

HOPING FOR A HARVEST OF SOULS

*"For when we were yet without strength, in due time Christ
died for the ungodly" (Romans 5:6 KJV).
"For we were saved in this hope" (Romans 8:24 NKJV).*

I remember asking someone years ago if he expected to get a job soon. He answered, "I hope so." I challenged him for using the word hope! I said, "You don't need hope. You need faith!" I was wrong. When the Bible says in 1 Corinthians 13 that faith, hope, and love abide, that means there is nothing wrong with saying "I hope so," because, as we said earlier, hope is an enduring quality. If you take away a person's hope, he can't apply his faith to anything. When the man said "I hope so," he was on the right track.

The whole chapter of Romans 8 describes the hope of believers who follow the Spirit of God. The word "hope" in Romans 8:24 means to anticipate with pleasure. It means having expectations and confidence as you face the future. People without hope move toward fatalism. They are headed in a negative direction just by being without hope. That's why we need to reach them with the Gospel.

Christians are the only ones who can realistically have hope. The rest of the world bases its hope on wishful thinking. Our hope is in God, the Creator of hope. It is centered on Jesus. It stands upon the eternal values of faith, hope, and love that abide forever.

God gives us not only a reason for living but the *right* reason for living and the assurance of His backing as we fulfill His will. Even if you don't like your job or you face other challenges daily, when you know God you still live with a sense of expectancy. You know that the Lord is with you. Your hope and confidence come from beliefs that are based on reality.

Your hope is strong when you first say, "I believe." Your hope gives you a reason to live. Even if you have done things wrong in the past, once you have chosen Jesus as your Savior you cross over into the dimension of eternal life where you can have hope for the future.

Jesus died for the ungodly. When a Christian tells an unsaved person that he can receive Jesus Christ as Lord and Savior, something supernatural happens as the Spirit of God gives him hope and a sense of purpose for his life.

That is something worth talking about.

THROUGH-THE-BIBLE IN ONE YEAR DAILY READING GUIDE

Fill in the four Bible chapters for today's date from the guide in the back of this journal.

Today's Four Bible Readings	My Personal Notes
_____	_____
_____	_____
_____	_____
_____	_____

MY PRAYER PRIORITIES FOR TODAY

My Right Relationship With God

_____
_____
_____

Leaders—Local, State, Nation, World

_____
_____
_____

Needs of Family and Friends

_____
_____
_____

Worldwide Revivals and Awakenings

_____
_____
_____

Five-Fold Ministry Church Leadership

_____
_____
_____

Praise and Thanksgiving

_____
_____
_____

HOPE FOR THE SINNER WHO HAS NO MORE STRENGTH

"The one thing that the poor strengthless sinner has to fix his mind upon, and firmly retain, as his one ground of hope, is the divine assurance that 'in due time Christ died for the ungodly.' Believe this, and all inability will disappear." —Charles Spurgeon (1834-1892)

MONEY MANAGEMENT AND WEALTH

_____ _____
_____ _____
_____ _____
_____ _____
_____ _____

"When we were utterly helpless, Christ came at just the right time and died for us sinners. . . . And since we have been made right in God's sight by the blood of Christ, he will certainly save us from God's judgment" (Romans 5:6,9).

MY TREASURE CHEST OF HOPE

Counting My Many Blessings   Planning My Hopes and Dreams

_____ _____
_____ _____
_____ _____
_____ _____
_____ _____
_____ _____
_____ _____

GREAT TESTIMONIES OF HOPE—CHARLES SPURGEON

Not condemned but saved

When Charles Spurgeon (1834-1892) was 19 years old, he preached his first message at London's New Park Street Church. At the time, 232 people were rattling around in a church built for 1500, but by the time of the evening service he was drawing a crowd. In a little over a year he was the most popular preacher in London. In 1861 he built Metropolitan Tabernacle that was supposed to seat 5,000 to 6,000 people, but they had to pack services with 7,000 and provide tickets to control the crowds.

Spurgeon was raised Congregationalist and became Baptist in 1850. He said, "I am never ashamed to avow myself a Calvinist; I do not hesitate to take the name of Baptist; but if I am asked what is my creed, I reply, 'It is Jesus Christ.' "

The following story gives an example of his influence.

"One evening he advised his people when they went home to get a sheet of paper and write on it either the word 'Saved' or the word 'Condemned.' A man whose wife and children were members of the church, who had only gone to the tabernacle to please them, took a sheet of paper when he went home and began to write the latter word. One of his daughters went up to him, put her arms round his neck and said, 'No, father, you shan't write that.' Her tears fell on the paper; the mother came up and pleaded with him; they all knelt in prayer together; and when he rose he put another curve to the letter C which he had written, turning it into an S, and then finished the word 'Saved.' "

LIFE OF CHARLES SPURGEON (1834-1892)

- *Made the most of every day.* Often worked 18-hour days.
- *Stood for truth.* Emphasized the cross and the Bible. Spoke out against error in the Church. Resigned from Baptist Union when they denied inerrancy of Scripture.
- *Evangelist.* Souls saved every day, including Oswald Chambers, who wrote *My Utmost for His Highest.*
- *Founded churches and ministries.* By 50th birthday had founded 66 organizations, including an orphanage.
- *Prolific writer and reader.* Sold 25,000 copies of his sermons weekly. His books and sermons were translated into 20 languages and fill 63 volumes.
- *Founded pastors' school.* He was primarily a pastor, and trained pastors in ministry. He taught them to persevere when all seemed against them.
- *Pressed through adversity.* First attack of gout at age 35; also rheumatism, kidney disease, and depression. Wife became an invalid confined to the home.
- *Endured criticism.* Area pastors spoke out publicly against him, which hurt him deeply, but he prayed that "the Lord would give me a short memory for grudges."

24-HOUR PERSONAL ACCOUNTABILITY JOURNAL
How I spent every hour of my life today

12 AM	
1 AM	
2 AM	
3 AM	
4 AM	
5 AM	
6 AM	
7 AM	
8 AM	
9 AM	
10 AM	
11 AM	
12 PM	
1 PM	
2 PM	
3 PM	
4 PM	
5 PM	
6 PM	
7 PM	
8 PM	
9 PM	
10 PM	
11 PM	

Today's Journal of Personal Insights

_____

_____

_____

_____

_____

_____

_____

_____

_____

_____

_____

_____

"Follow peace with all men, and holiness,
without which no man shall see the Lord" (Hebrews 12:14 KJV).

My Self-Evaluation—How Well Did I Do Today?

You may grade yourself as you rate your day. This is between you and God.

❏ Praise, worship, and thanksgiving   ❏ Family time

❏ Prayer and extraordinary prayer   ❏ Time with friends

❏ Reading and meditating on the Word of God   ❏ Reaching the lost

❏ Fasting and other sacrifices   ❏ Eating right and exercising

❏ Serving others in Christ-like love   ❏ Organizing myself to serve God

"The eyes of your understanding being enlightened;
that ye may know what is the hope of his calling,
and what the riches of the glory of his inheritance in the saints"
(Ephesians 1:18 KJV).

Only 13 days to go in your *Countdown to Hope.*

CHANGING SOCIETY BY HOPE

"May your will be done here on earth,
just as it is in heaven" (Matthew 6:10).
". . . as he is, so are we in this world" (1 John 4:17 KJV).

Two centuries ago a young British statesman named William
Wilberforce set out to accomplish two goals: the reformation of
society and the abolition of slavery. He fulfilled those hopes.

Christians today have become incompetent at changing society
with that level of zeal because we have forgotten that God is counting on
us, His people, to change the world by His power.

You can do anything that God can do because the DNA qualities
of God are in your seed. As you use this journal, you will discover some
places in you that are not like God. Identify your areas of wrong thinking
and cast them down. Throw out everything that does not match God's
DNA until all that is left inside of you is hope.

Some dark seeds of failure and hopelessness follow family lines
for generations. Seeds of oppression and murder. Sickness and disease.
Wrong thinking. Inappropriate sexual behavior. Those seeds are not
ordained to grow. God sent another seed through His Son. Mary's
immaculate conception demonstrated God's potential to accomplish
anything He wants in people who yield fully to His will.

Hebrews 12:2 (KJV) says, "Looking unto Jesus the author and
finisher of our faith." When we see Jesus and realize that He is in us, we
have hope that we can change our thinking and transform society. When
God told Adam, "Be fruitful, multiply, and replenish the earth" (Genesis
1:28 KJV), by definition He was speaking over him the God-like power to
expand and improve things everywhere he went. That is God's nature;
therefore, that is *our* nature.

Anyone who resists God will lose, because God is all powerful.
Anyone who resists us cannot succeed either, because God is in us, and "as
he is, so are we in this world" (1 John 4:17).

When God said, "Let us make man after Our image and likeness,"
He was saying, "I am willing to be identified *in* My creation" and "I am
willing to be identified *as* My creation. The world doesn't realize that it
has only one hope left—Christians who do whatever is necessary to purify
themselves, become like Jesus, and use their influence to bring change by
introducing people to their Lord and Savior.

THROUGH-THE-BIBLE IN ONE YEAR DAILY READING GUIDE

Fill in the four Bible chapters for today's date from the guide in the back of this journal.

Today's Four Bible Readings	My Personal Notes
☐ _____	_____
☐ _____	_____
☐ _____	_____
☐ _____	_____

MY PRAYER PRIORITIES FOR TODAY

My Right Relationship With God
_____
_____
_____

Leaders—Local, State, Nation, World
_____
_____
_____

Needs of Family and Friends
_____
_____
_____

Worldwide Revivals and Awakenings
_____
_____
_____

Five-Fold Ministry Church Leadership
_____
_____
_____

Praise and Thanksgiving
_____
_____
_____

GOD'S BLESSING COVERS YOU WHEN YOU'RE IN THE RIGHT PLACE

". . . if I were thus to fly from the post where Providence has placed me, I know not how I could look for the blessing of God upon my retirement: and without this heavenly assistance, either in the world or in solitude our own endeavors will be equally ineffectual." —William Wilberforce (1759-1833)

MONEY MANAGEMENT AND WEALTH

_____   _____
_____   _____
_____   _____
_____   _____

". . . money answereth all things" (Ecclesiastes 10:19 KJV).

MY TREASURE CHEST OF HOPE

Counting My Many Blessings   Planning My Hopes and Dreams

_____   _____
_____   _____
_____   _____
_____   _____
_____   _____
_____   _____
_____   _____

GREAT TESTIMONIES OF HOPE—WILLIAM WILBERFORCE

Godly influence on people and nations

In 1780, William Wilberforce (1759-1833) was elected a member of the British Parliament. He was 21 years old, and he had carried the election on his natural ability to win people. He didn't know it at the time, but he was going to need all of that relational ability for defeating one of the greatest evils of his day, the British slave trade.

Four years later, Wilberforce, whose family was very wealthy, went to the French Riviera with his family and friends. It was a turning point in his life. Through conversations with his friend Isaac Milnor, an evangelical Methodist, and by reading a book by Philip Doddridge called *The Rise and Progress of Religion in the Soul* (1745), he became convinced that his wealth and power had left him empty. It pained him to realize that he had been practicing a superficial form of Christianity. He had failed to become a true radical for Christ.

He wrote in his journal, "Often while in the full enjoyment of all that this world could bestow, my conscience told me that in the true sense of the word, I was not a Christian. I laughed, I sang, I was apparently gay and happy, but the thought would steal across me, 'What madness is all this.'"

Out of this spiritual travail was birthed a man of God, an unlikely leader of the nation's Christians in the public arena. He was short and somewhat deformed, but also eloquent and extremely bright. Combined with an awakened consecration he was hard to beat.

After rediscovering the extreme faith that he had heard about as a child from John Newton (1725-1807), the evangelical pastor and ex-slave trader who wrote the song "Amazing Grace," and from his aunt and uncle, who were friends of revivalist George Whitefield, he thought that he should leave his position in government. However, Newton and William Pitt, his college buddy who became England's youngest Prime Minister, persuaded him to stay in Parliament.

As a result, Wilberforce had a remarkable influence on world history. His tireless efforts brought about an end to slavery in the British Empire almost 30 years before the American Civil War. He was one of the first leaders to see slavery not as an economic necessity but as sin, which was the same change of mindset that was coming to the American abolitionists through evangelist Charles Finney and others.

Wilberforce's greatest desire was not only to be personally right with God but also to bring his nation into right relationship with Him. His journal for the summer of 1786 reveals his search for Christian discipline and a clear "God-said" for his life. He said, "God Almighty has set before me two great objects, the suppression of the slave trade and the reformation of manners" (a term meaning to restore virtue to public life). That was to become his life's work.

Wilberforce gathered around him notable Christians of his day and they formed what became the "Clapham Sect," named for the town where Wilberforce lived. Its members included Thomas Clarkson, Edward James Eliot, Charles Grant, Zachary Macaulay, Hannah More, Granville Sharp, James Stephen, and Henry Thornton. They were distinguished leaders in their own right and became energized by Wilberforce's hope that they could win. During his lifetime, they brought breakthroughs in nearly 70 different social causes—all in the name of Christ.

24-HOUR PERSONAL ACCOUNTABILITY JOURNAL
How I spent every hour of my life today

12 AM	
1 AM	
2 AM	
3 AM	
4 AM	
5 AM	
6 AM	
7 AM	
8 AM	
9 AM	
10 AM	
11 AM	
12 PM	
1 PM	
2 PM	
3 PM	
4 PM	
5 PM	
6 PM	
7 PM	
8 PM	
9 PM	
10 PM	
11 PM	

_____

_____

_____

_____

_____

_____

_____

_____

_____

_____

"Dear friends, if our conscience is clear, we can come to God with bold confidence. And we will receive whatever we request because we obey him and do the things that please him" (1 John 3:21-22).

MY SELF-EVALUATION—HOW WELL DID I DO TODAY?

You may grade yourself as you rate your day. This is between you and God.

❑ Praise, worship, and thanksgiving   ❑ Family time

❑ Prayer and extraordinary prayer   ❑ Time with friends

❑ Reading and meditating on the Word of God   ❑ Reaching the lost

❑ Fasting and other sacrifices   ❑ Eating right and exercising

❑ Serving others in Christ-like love   ❑ Organizing myself to serve God

"Every king in all the earth will give you thanks, O LORD, for all of them will hear your words. Yes, they will sing about the LORD's ways, for the glory of the LORD is very great" (Psalm 138:4-5).

Only 12 days to go in your *Countdown to Hope.*

REPLENISHING HOPE OF THE POOR

"And God blessed them, and God said unto them, Be fruitful,
and multiply, and replenish the earth, and subdue it"
(Genesis 1:28 KJV).

Hope is providential. It speaks of fruitfulness, multiplication, and growth. Maybe you don't have a job yet, but you went to college to prepare for one. Maybe you already have a job, but you are preparing for the next one you hope to have. You are always moving in an advancement mode toward something better. It is not because you are a malcontent, but you press forward because the Bible emphasizes increase.

What words has God spoken that you hope will come to pass? Let me give you a few examples. You hope you are going to heaven. You hope you are not going to hell. If you are married, you hope you will have a great marriage. If you are single, you hope you will find a great mate. You hope to go to college and do well. You hope you will not be poor.

Do you have any "God said's" that you could build your life upon? Have you documented any hopes in your Treasure Chest of Hope in this journal? Keep your hope alive with words that describe your vision.

When God placed Adam in the Garden, Adam's most important responsibility was to tend the *words* that God had spoken to him. His first jurisdictional responsibility was to tend the garden of his understanding. God gave him authority over the whole earth, but the Bible says that Adam tended the Garden.

When God made man, it was a win-win situation. God was going to win and man was going to win. God knew the devil would come in and challenge His words, because he was evil and everything good was held together by God's standard. If man had kept God's standard, the benefits would have continued for all living beings to come. Negatives would not have existed. Nobody would have had to worry about lying, stealing, and murder. When God said, "Be fruitful, multiply, and replenish the earth," He was declaring that one man's good seed would dominate the whole earth. Everybody would prosper as a product of who Adam was in God.

Adam hijacked the potential God gave him that was to benefit everyone who came after him, based on the word of God inside. Are you tending the Word of God inside you? Are you tending hope? Are you fruitful with hope? Do you multiply hope in others? Or has the devil stolen God's words in you and caused you to turn away and hide?

Choose to tend your garden of hope today. Be fruitful, multiply, and replenish the seed of hope in everyone, everywhere you go.

THROUGH-THE-BIBLE IN ONE YEAR DAILY READING GUIDE
Fill in the four Bible chapters for today's date from the guide in the back of this journal.

Today's Four Bible Readings	My Personal Notes
☐ _____	_____
☐ _____	_____
☐ _____	_____
☐ _____	_____

MY PRAYER PRIORITIES FOR TODAY

My Right Relationship With God
_____
_____
_____
_____

Leaders—Local, State, Nation, World
_____
_____
_____
_____

Needs of Family and Friends
_____
_____
_____
_____

Worldwide Revivals and Awakenings
_____
_____
_____
_____

Five-Fold Ministry Church Leadership
_____
_____
_____
_____

Praise and Thanksgiving
_____
_____
_____
_____

GOD UNLOCKED A MYSTERY AND THE POOR RECEIVED HOPE

"When I was young, I said to God, God, tell me the mystery of the universe. But God answered, that knowledge is for me alone. So I said, God, tell me the mystery of the peanut. Then God said, well, George, that's more nearly your size."
—George Washington Carver (1864-1943) who developed more than 300 uses for peanuts

MONEY MANAGEMENT AND WEALTH

*"I helped those without hope, and they blessed me. And I
caused the widows' hearts to sing for joy" (Job 29:13).*

MY TREASURE CHEST OF HOPE

Counting My Many Blessings   Planning My Hopes and Dreams

GREAT TESTIMONIES OF HOPE—GEORGE WASHINGTON CARVER

Sowing seeds of progress because of faith in the Creator

George Washington Carver (1864-1943) was a former slave who
became not only the world's foremost expert on peanuts and sweet
potatoes but also a man of faith in God who sowed hope for progress
among struggling Southern farmers after the Civil War.

Carver's mother Mary was only 13 when she was purchased by a
slave master named Moses Carver during the Civil War. She died while
George was still a child. Although he was an orphan and often suffered
from poor health, he loved to learn and educated himself at every
opportunity. He had a special love for botany and was called "The Plant
Doctor" even as a boy. He said later, "My very soul thirsted for an
education. I literally lived in the woods. I wanted to know every strange
stone, flower, insect, bird, or beast."

Carver became famous not only for his research but also for his openness about crediting "Mr. Creator" for all of his discoveries. He told a New York City audience, "I never have to grope for methods. The method is revealed at the moment I am inspired to create something new. . . . Without God to draw aside the curtain I would be helpless."

When the *New York Times* heard about his faith, it published an editorial called "Men of Science Never Talk that Way." They criticized Carver for referencing God instead of evolution, but he didn't back down. He kept quoting Scripture. He said, "I regret exceedingly that such a gross misunderstanding should arise as to what was meant by 'Divine inspiration.' Inspiration is never at variance with information; in fact, the more information one has, the greater will be the inspiration."

Carver said that God allowed him "often many times per day to permit me to speak to him through the three great Kingdoms of the world, which he has created, viz. —the Animal, Mineral, and Vegetable Kingdoms; their relations to each other, to us, our relations to them and the Great God who made all of us."

Although he graduated from what is now Iowa State and could have had a career on the faculty there, he chose instead to accept the invitation of Booker T. Washington to head the new Department of Agriculture at Tuskegee Institute where Black students could be educated. He served there faithfully for 47 years.

From his base at Tuskegee he gave hope to children of slaves and slave masters in the South that they could grow new crops instead of cotton, which had depleted the soil and was largely destroyed by the boll weevil in the early 20th century. He focused on developing self-sufficiency in poor farmers struggling to be independent and take care of their families.

Carver developed:

- *More than 300 products from peanuts*
- *More than 100 uses for the sweet potato*
- *Free educational bulletins with advice on livestock, soil improvement, cultivation, and nutritious recipes from crops*
- *The Jessup Wagon, a demonstration laboratory on wheels that he used to further educate farmers*

The George Washington Carver National Monument was established by an act of Congress in July 1943 after his death. It includes 210 acres of the original farm where he was once a slave.

His willingness to stand for God and sow hope in the poor through faith and science is still admired today even by skeptics. That is a worthy legacy.

24-HOUR PERSONAL ACCOUNTABILITY JOURNAL
How I spent every hour of my life today

12 AM	
1 AM	
2 AM	
3 AM	
4 AM	
5 AM	
6 AM	
7 AM	
8 AM	
9 AM	
10 AM	
11 AM	
12 PM	
1 PM	
2 PM	
3 PM	
4 PM	
5 PM	
6 PM	
7 PM	
8 PM	
9 PM	
10 PM	
11 PM	

TODAY'S JOURNAL OF PERSONAL INSIGHTS

_____

_____

_____

_____

_____

_____

_____

_____

_____

_____

_____

_____

_____

"If you obey all the laws and commands that I will give you today, all will be well with you and your children. Then you will enjoy a long life in the land the LORD your God is giving you for all time" (Deuteronomy 4:40).

MY SELF-EVALUATION—HOW WELL DID I DO TODAY?

You may grade yourself as you rate your day. This is between you and God.

❑ Praise, worship, and thanksgiving   ❑ Family time

❑ Prayer and extraordinary prayer   ❑ Time with friends

❑ Reading and meditating on the Word of God   ❑ Reaching the lost

❑ Fasting and other sacrifices   ❑ Eating right and exercising

❑ Serving others in Christ-like love   ❑ Organizing myself to serve God

"Look at those who are honest and good, for a wonderful future lies before those who love peace" (Psalm 37:37).

Only 11 days to go in your *Countdown to Hope.*

PRAYING FOR HOPELESS SINNERS

"The thought of my suffering and homelessness is bitter beyond words. I will never forget this awful time, as I grieve over my loss. Yet I still dare to hope" (Lamentations 3:19-21).

When Jeremiah considered how people had rejected him he said, "The thought of . . . my homelessness is bitter beyond words." We might never think of a prophet in the Bible as being homeless, but he was. I don't know a single Christian who would get so excited about looking for a prophecy from a homeless person that he would look under bridges and search the alleys to find one. The Bible gives us hope that we can hear from God even if we are homeless because God will use anyone He chooses under any circumstances.

During Charles Finney's crusade in Evans Mill, New York, that you read about earlier, Finney met a man of prayer named Father Nash who had enough hope to pray for the worst sinners in the city. Together they were convinced that God wanted to bring a transformation to that region. They would not rest until they saw a new city.

The Bible says in Hebrews 11:10, "Abraham was confidently looking forward to a city with eternal foundations, a city designed and built by God." In the King James Version it says that Abraham looked for a city "whose builder and maker was God."

The Bible presents a track record of patriarchs who give us hope that we can hear from God. Abraham heard from God in a way that no one he knew had ever experienced. There was no basis for his faith other than his divine connection with God. He followed a path that God showed him.

You have been born again into a new world. God can unveil to you in a dimension of the spirit something you never thought of before. He can give you hope for people you never even considered as someone who could be saved. He will open up heaven to you and you will find yourself looking forward to something that just never came to your mind before.

Every born again believer has a seed of hope inside, not only for themselves but also for hopeless sinners. We have the DNA structure to be people of faith. Faith is the engine that drives us to hope for the impossible.

Remember, Abraham hoped against hope. When the Lord told him he would have a son and heir, in the natural he had nothing to hope about. However, he had the assurance that the Lord's will would come to pass. He had reason to hope because of the veracity of God's Word.

You may not see a solution to your situation. All your plans may be dead, but just follow the lead of the Author and Finisher of your faith.

Through-the-Bible in One Year Daily Reading Guide

Fill in the four Bible chapters for today's date from the guide in the back of this journal.

Today's Four Bible Readings	My Personal Notes
☐ _____	_____
☐ _____	_____
☐ _____	_____
☐ _____	_____

My Prayer Priorities for Today

My Right Relationship With God
_____
_____
_____

Leaders—Local, State, Nation, World
_____
_____
_____

Needs of Family and Friends
_____
_____
_____

Worldwide Revivals and Awakenings
_____
_____
_____

Five-Fold Ministry Church Leadership
_____
_____
_____

Praise and Thanksgiving
_____
_____
_____

Earnest, Devout, and Effective in Praying for Sinners

Father Daniel Nash "was a most wonderful man in prayer, one of the most earnest, devout, spiritually-minded, heavenly-minded men I ever saw. . . . He labored about in many places in central and northern New York, and gave himself up to almost constant prayer, literally praying himself to death at last.
I have been informed that he was found dead in his room in the attitude of prayer."
—Charles Finney's words about Daniel Nash (1775-1831), his chief intercessor
Finney credited to prayer the fact that 80 percent of his converts remained faithful to Christ.

MONEY MANAGEMENT AND WEALTH

_____   _____
_____   _____
_____   _____
_____   _____
_____   _____

"The princess of Tyre will shower you with gifts. The wealthy will beg your favor.
. . . Your sons will become kings like their father.
You will make them rulers over many lands" (Psalm 45:12,16).

MY TREASURE CHEST OF HOPE

Counting My Many Blessings   Planning My Hopes and Dreams

_____   _____
_____   _____
_____   _____
_____   _____
_____   _____
_____   _____
_____   _____
_____   _____
_____   _____

GREAT TESTIMONIES OF HOPE—FATHER NASH

Profession of hope transforms a bar into a prayer room

Charles Finney wrote in his *Memoirs* about a remarkable man of
prayer who began to labor with him for revival at Evans Mills, New York.
Through the prayers of Daniel Nash the town reprobate found hope in
Christ and a community was transformed. Here is Father Nash's story.

> *"After he was at presbytery he was taken with inflamed eyes; and*
> *for several weeks was shut up in a dark room. He could neither*
> *read nor write, and, as I learned, gave himself up almost entirely*
> *to prayer. He had a terrible overhauling in his whole Christian*
> *experience; and as soon as he was able to see, with a double*
> *black veil before his face, he sallied forth to labor for souls.*
> *"When he came to Evans' Mills he was full of the power*

of prayer. He was another man altogether from what he had been at any former period of his Christian life. I found that he had a praying list, as he called it, of the names of persons whom he made subjects of prayer every day, and sometimes many times a day. And praying with him, and hearing him pray in meeting, I found that his gift of prayer was wonderful, and his faith almost miraculous.

"There was a man by the name of D, who kept a low tavern in a corner of the village, whose house was the resort of all the opposers of the revival. The barroom was a place of blasphemy; and he was himself a most profane, ungodly; abusive man. He went railing about the streets respecting the revival; and would take particular pains to swear and blaspheme whenever he saw a Christian. . . . He had not, I think, been at any of our meetings. Of course he was ignorant of the great truths of religion, and despised the whole Christian enterprise.

"Father Nash heard us speak of this Mr. D as a hard case; and immediately put his name upon his praying list. He remained in town a day or two, and went on his way, having in view another field of labor.

"Not many days afterward, as we were holding an evening meeting with a very crowded house, who should come in but this notorious D? His entrance created a considerable movement in the congregation. People feared that he had come in to make a disturbance. The fear and abhorrence of him had become very general among Christians, I believe; so that when he came in, some of the people got up and retired. I knew his countenance, and kept my eye upon him; I very soon became satisfied that he had not come in to oppose, and that he was in great anguish of mind. He sat and writhed upon his seat, and was very uneasy. He soon arose, and tremblingly asked me if he might say a few words. I told him that he might. He then proceeded to make one of the most heart-broken confessions that I almost ever heard. His confession seemed to cover the whole ground of his treatment of God, and of his treatment of Christians, and of the revival, and of everything good.

"This thoroughly broke up the fallow ground in many hearts. It was the most powerful means that could have been used, just then, to give an impetus to the work. D soon came out and professed a hope, abolished all the revelry and profanity of his barroom; and from that time, as long as I stayed there, and I know not how much longer, a prayer meeting was held in his barroom nearly every night."

24-HOUR PERSONAL ACCOUNTABILITY JOURNAL
How I spent every hour of my life today

12 AM	
1 AM	
2 AM	
3 AM	
4 AM	
5 AM	
6 AM	
7 AM	
8 AM	
9 AM	
10 AM	
11 AM	
12 PM	
1 PM	
2 PM	
3 PM	
4 PM	
5 PM	
6 PM	
7 PM	
8 PM	
9 PM	
10 PM	
11 PM	

TODAY'S JOURNAL OF PERSONAL INSIGHTS

_____

_____

_____

_____

_____

_____

_____

_____

_____

_____

_____

_____

_____

"Yes, dear friends, we are already God's children, and we can't even imagine what we will be like when Christ returns. But we do know that when he comes we will be like him, for we will see him as he really is. And all who believe this will keep themselves pure, just as Christ is pure" (1 John 3:2-3).

MY SELF-EVALUATION—HOW WELL DID I DO TODAY?

You may grade yourself as you rate your day. This is between you and God.

❑ Praise, worship, and thanksgiving   ❑ Family time

❑ Prayer and extraordinary prayer   ❑ Time with friends

❑ Reading and meditating on the Word of God   ❑ Reaching the lost

❑ Fasting and other sacrifices   ❑ Eating right and exercising

❑ Serving others in Christ-like love   ❑ Organizing myself to serve God

"For all creation is waiting eagerly for that future day when God will reveal who his children really are" (Romans 8:18-19).

Only 10 days to go in your *Countdown to Hope.*

PREACHING HOPE FROM A WAREHOUSE

"The harvest is so great, but the workers are so few.
Pray to the Lord who is in charge of the harvest,
and ask him to send out more workers for his fields"
(Luke 10:2).

Some day I believe that we will hear in heaven that the prayers of godly people have been carrying this nation even more than their labor. Intercessors pray all night. They fast. They seek God until He comes. God is calling them back to their dedication.

Before I was saved and I was still in the world, I thought nothing of staying out late on Friday night to party. Now I am more committed to staying up late to pray than I was to serving sin and the devil. The people around me are the same way.

Prayer is the key to what is about to happen. Prayer is our strength and the source of our power to lead and serve others. Prayer lays the tracks. We pray there before we go there, in effect laying the tracks for revival.

William Seymour was a Black intercessor and pastor seeking God when an outpouring of the Holy Spirit at the simple warehouse where he was holding meetings launched a worldwide movement. My church currently meets in a renovated warehouse. We call it "The Hope Warehouse" because hope lives there. We spread hope from the place where God is.

When you become personally consecrated, you can hear from God anywhere and you can create an environment where people will come who are seeking Him. You can increase your ability to hear God's voice through your dedication and prayers for others.

Hearing God clearly is an inevitable result of the process of consecration. You may not have the power to change society yet, but you can change yourself through your commitment to consecration. Then you can hear God when He tells you how to lead.

That is the message that God wants to give the Church.

You may be hampered by prejudice. You may have issues with unrighteous laws, but God can come in a moment and change everything. You just have to remain faithful to your calling. You have to stay in hope.

THROUGH-THE-BIBLE IN ONE YEAR DAILY READING GUIDE

Fill in the four Bible chapters for today's date from the guide in the back of this journal.

Today's Four Bible Readings	My Personal Notes
☐ _____	_____
☐ _____	_____
☐ _____	_____
☐ _____	_____

MY PRAYER PRIORITIES FOR TODAY

My Right Relationship With God

_____
_____
_____

Leaders—Local, State, Nation, World

_____
_____
_____

Needs of Family and Friends

_____
_____
_____

Worldwide Revivals and Awakenings

_____
_____
_____

Five-Fold Ministry Church Leadership

_____
_____
_____

Praise and Thanksgiving

_____
_____
_____

THIS MAN A GIFT TO THE WHOLE BODY OF CHRIST

" 'We belong to the whole body of Christ' is a phrase that might well be applied to the band of worshipers who gathered together in the Azusa Street Mission in April of 1906. . . . Seymour cannot be claimed only by the blacks, or the Pentecostals; he belongs to the whole body of Christ—of all nations, races, and peoples. And the baptism in the Holy Spirit, with the accompanying gifts and graces does not belong only to the Pentecostals, but to the whole body of Christ—indeed unto 'as many as the Lord our God shall call' (Acts 2:39)."
— Frank Bartleman (1871-1936), minister and unofficial historian of Azusa Street revival

MONEY MANAGEMENT AND WEALTH

_____   _____
_____   _____
_____   _____
_____   _____
_____   _____

"Why should I fear when trouble comes, when enemies surround me?
They trust in their wealth and boast of great riches. Yet they cannot
redeem themselves from death by paying a ransom to God. Redemption does not
come so easily, for no one can ever pay enough to live forever" (Psalm 49:5-8).

MY TREASURE CHEST OF HOPE

Counting My Many Blessings   Planning My Hopes and Dreams
_____   _____
_____   _____
_____   _____
_____   _____
_____   _____
_____   _____
_____   _____
_____   _____

GREAT TESTIMONIES OF HOPE—WILLIAM SEYMOUR

Church with few resources in former warehouse reaches the world

William Seymour (1870-1922), a Black preacher blind in one eye,
began holding revival meetings in a simple warehouse at Azusa Street in
Los Angeles a century ago. He called it the Apostolic Faith Mission.
Seymour was the son of former slaves and he shared their simple faith. As
he and a few other faithful people were seeking God, the Holy Spirit fell
on them as at Pentecost and they began to speak in tongues. Out of their
passion for God they started a church in the only building they could afford
and their impact eventually reached the world.

The building at Azusa Street had been a warehouse and had
recently been used as a stable, like Jesus' birthplace. Seymour and a small
group of Blacks who were with him pitched in and cleaned it up. The seats
were made of planks and the pulpit consisted of wooden crates, but

eventually as many as 600 people of all races would crowd inside a space only 40 by 60 feet, with hundreds more outside. The walls were lined with crutches and wheelchairs no longer needed after people were healed. Thousands of people came from everywhere.

C. H. Mason, founder of the Church of God in Christ, went there to find out about the baptism of the Holy Spirit with the evidence of speaking in tongues. He said, "The first day in the meeting I sat to myself, away from those that went with me. I began to thank God in my heart for all things, for when I heard some speak in tongues, I knew it was right, though I did not understand it. Nevertheless, it was sweet to me."

Miraculously, in a day of racial prejudice, many of the people who came were White. Some eventually founded denominations like the Assemblies of God that have reached millions.

Church historian Vinson Synan wrote, "What happened at Azusa Street during the next three years was to change the course of church history. . . . The central attraction was tongues, with the addition of traditional Black worship styles that included shouting, trances, and the holy dance. There was no order of service, since 'the Holy Ghost was in control.' No offerings were taken, although a box hung on the wall proclaimed, 'Settle with the Lord.' Altar workers enthusiastically prayed with seekers. It was a noisy place, and services lasted into the night.

"Though local newspaper coverage spoke cynically about the 'weird babble of tongues' of 'colored mammys,' on street corners and trolley cars, the news intrigued the city. Whole congregations came en masse to Azusa Street and stayed while their former churches disappeared. Other Pentecostal centers soon sprang up around town."

While attending the Azusa Street meetings, Mason was filled with the Holy Spirit and began to speak in tongues. Seymour considered tongues to be a sign of unity, like the day of Pentecost, crossing racial lines. He said, "Don't go out of here talking about tongues: talk about Jesus." Frank Bartleman, a minister and historian of the movement, said, "The color line has been washed away in the Blood."

For more than three years the Apostolic Faith Mission at Azusa Street met three times a day, seven days a week. The results have increased exponentially worldwide since that time.

Whether your church meets in a cathedral, a stable or a warehouse, hope that God will bless your dedication with results as great as theirs. It's not the size of the building that matters, but the enlargement of your heart.

24-HOUR PERSONAL ACCOUNTABILITY JOURNAL
How I spent every hour of my life today

12 AM	
1 AM	
2 AM	
3 AM	
4 AM	
5 AM	
6 AM	
7 AM	
8 AM	
9 AM	
10 AM	
11 AM	
12 PM	
1 PM	
2 PM	
3 PM	
4 PM	
5 PM	
6 PM	
7 PM	
8 PM	
9 PM	
10 PM	
11 PM	

_____

_____

_____

_____

_____

_____

_____

_____

_____

_____

_____

"God overlooked people's ignorance about these things in earlier times, but now he commands everyone everywhere to repent of their sins and turn to him. For he has set a day for judging the world with justice by the man he has appointed, and he proved to everyone who this is by raising him from the dead" (Acts 17:30-31).

MY SELF-EVALUATION—HOW WELL DID I DO TODAY?

You may grade yourself as you rate your day. This is between you and God.

❑ Praise, worship, and thanksgiving   ❑ Family time

❑ Prayer and extraordinary prayer   ❑ Time with friends

❑ Reading and meditating on the Word of God   ❑ Reaching the lost

❑ Fasting and other sacrifices   ❑ Eating right and exercising

❑ Serving others in Christ-like love   ❑ Organizing myself to serve God

"For the Lord himself will come down from heaven with a commanding shout, with the call of the archangel, and with the trumpet call of God. First, all the Christians who have died will rise from their graves. Then, together with them, we who are still alive and remain on the earth will be caught up in the clouds to meet the Lord in the air and remain with him forever" (1 Thessalonians 4:16-17).

Only 9 days to go in your *Countdown to Hope.*

DAY 22. _____ *(date)*

INSPIRING HOPE BY WRITING

*"And the one sitting on the throne said, 'Look, I am making all
things new!' And then he said to me, 'Write this down, for what
I tell you is trustworthy and true.' And he also said, 'It is
finished! I am the Alpha and the Omega—the Beginning and
the End' " (Revelation 21:5-6).*

"Write this down," Jesus told John. "Write this down, for what I tell
you is trustworthy and true." This is what you believe when you
start a journal—that God will tell you things that are trustworthy and true
and He expects you to write them down. Why should you write them
down? Because it is so easy to forget the revelations of the moment and
when God gives you insights He wants you to remember them.

Sometimes God gives me insights that I know are just for myself.
He might give me permission to share them or He might not. They are the
fruit of my intimacy with God. Writing things down says they are
important enough to keep. I don't take God's words for granted. He
doesn't speak to everyone and He doesn't speak to me all the time.
Sometimes I am in a time of prayer somewhere and sometimes I am not
and He just drops things on me.

As a pastor, I know that many of the things God tells me are for
ministry and teaching others through preaching and writing. Every minister
believes that in some way he is seeking God not only for himself but also
for others. God makes all things new. Could you dare to hope that God will
say something new to you that will change other people's lives when they
hear it? Wouldn't it be provident to write down those words?

Jesus said, "When the Spirit of truth comes, he will guide you into
all truth. He will not be presenting his own ideas; he will be telling you
what he has heard. He will tell you about the future. He will bring me glory
by revealing to you whatever he receives from me" (John 16:13-14).

God will reveal whole new dimensions of leadership to you if you
will become His representative on earth right now. Dedicate yourself for
the rest of your life to becoming more like Him and doing what God has
ordained. The Holy Spirit is working on your behalf. Believe in God. Hope
that your prayers will make difference. Ask God to reveal His mind and
heart and keep your heart tender as you write in your journal.

He said, "To all who are thirsty I will give the springs of the water
of life without charge! All who are victorious will inherit all these
blessings, and I will be their God, and they will be my children"
(Revelation 21:6-7).

THROUGH-THE-BIBLE IN ONE YEAR DAILY READING GUIDE

Fill in the four Bible chapters for today's date from the guide in the back of this journal.

Today's Four Bible Readings	My Personal Notes
☐ _____	_____
☐ _____	_____
☐ _____	_____
☐ _____	_____

MY PRAYER PRIORITIES FOR TODAY

My Right Relationship With God

_____
_____
_____

Leaders—Local, State, Nation, World

_____
_____
_____

Needs of Family and Friends

_____
_____
_____

Worldwide Revivals and Awakenings

_____
_____
_____

Five-Fold Ministry Church Leadership

_____
_____
_____

Praise and Thanksgiving

_____
_____
_____

UNCLE TOM—FICTIONAL CHARACTER REPRESENTING CHRIST

" 'If I must be sold, or all the people on the place, and everything go to rack, why,
let me be sold. I s'pose I can b'ar it as well as any on 'em,' he added, while
something like a sob and a sigh shook his broad, rough chest convulsively. 'Mas'r
always found me on the spot,—he always will. I never have broke trust, nor used
my pass no ways contrary to my word, and I never will.
It 's better for me alone to go, than to break up the place and sell all.' "
—Fictional character Uncle Tom about his willingness to be sold as a slave to save others
From *Uncle Tom's Cabin* by Harriet Beecher Stowe (1811-1896)

24-HOUR PERSONAL ACCOUNTABILITY JOURNAL
How I spent every hour of my life today

12 AM	
1 AM	
2 AM	
3 AM	
4 AM	
5 AM	
6 AM	
7 AM	
8 AM	
9 AM	
10 AM	
11 AM	
12 PM	
1 PM	
2 PM	
3 PM	
4 PM	
5 PM	
6 PM	
7 PM	
8 PM	
9 PM	
10 PM	
11 PM	

MONEY MANAGEMENT AND WEALTH

_____   _____
_____   _____
_____   _____
_____   _____
_____   _____

"So God has given us both his promise and his oath. These two things are unchangeable because it is impossible for God to lie. Therefore, we who have fled to him for refuge can take new courage, for we can hold on to his promise with confidence" (Hebrews 6:18).

MY TREASURE CHEST OF HOPE

Counting My Many Blessings   Planning My Hopes and Dreams

_____   _____
_____   _____
_____   _____
_____   _____
_____   _____
_____   _____
_____   _____
_____   _____

GREAT TESTIMONIES OF HOPE—HARRIET BEECHER STOWE

Driven by the hope that her writing could help end slavery

In 1850, Harriet Beecher Stowe was a 39-year-old New England housewife when the North entered into an agreement to capture slaves escaping from the South. Provoked by the cruel captures that resulted from the Fugitive Slave Law, this daughter of the famous preacher Lyman Beecher cried out, "I will write something. I will write if I live!"

Her chapters were published first as a series of articles in the abolitionist paper *National Era*. When the full book was published, this work of fiction, *Uncle Tom's Cabin*, became an instant best-seller. Even today it is well-known as a power-packed anti-slavery treatise—except in the Black community, where the content of the book is hardly known at all, but the name "Uncle Tom" has become deeply hated.

Who was the real Uncle Tom? Significantly, this fictional character—who was based on a composite of real-life stories—was a Christ-like figure of compassion and high integrity who, as a suffering slave, refused to lie or break trust and then laid down his life so that other slaves could live.

This book was strong medicine for pre-Civil War America. Like Stowe's contemporaries, evangelist Charles Finney and Christian businessmen Arthur and Lewis Tappan, whose commitment to Christ drove them to seek social change, she used her writing skills to awaken the nation to see slavery as a sin. As an author and commentator within the book, she repeatedly challenges the reader to view slavery as something so terrible that the conscience of any thinking Christian—North or South—must drive them to reject it and work toward its end.

People of America and other nations were forced to pay attention when they read the gripping accounts in *Uncle Tom's Cabin* and they changed their minds about slavery based solely on the impact of her words.

Author and cynic Heinrich Heine wrote, "Astonishing that after I have whirled about all my life over all the dance floors of philosophy and yielded myself to all the orgies of the intellect and paid my addresses to all possible systems without satisfaction, like Messaline after a licentious night, I now find myself on the same standpoint where poor Uncle Tom stands—on that of the Bible."

Uncle Tom's Cabin was originally intended to run for three months, but the newspaper serialization ran for ten. When the complete book was published in March 1852, within three months Mrs. Stowe had earned the incredible sum of $10,000, and within a year 300,000 copies had been sold.

At the time when she wrote her articles for *National Era*, most people in the North read newspapers voraciously. Countless thousands responded to her strong moral tone and they emotionally identified with the life-and-death struggles of her slave characters and their secret rescuers, such as the Quakers. They read the story aloud to their families.

However, because she took a strong position on such a controversial subject, many others strongly opposed her, accusing her of being untruthful, dangerous, and a poor writer. In response, she published an extensive documentation of the actual true-life events on which she based her story. It is called *Key to Uncle Tom's Cabin*.

Abraham Lincoln, commenting on the impact of *Uncle Tom's Cabin* on the course of history, said that Stowe was "the little woman who started this great [Civil] war." She was a crusading woman when it was not fashionable to be one, yet her compassion and sense of family proved to be some of her best attributes. She is a model for us, whether male or female, Black or White, as someone who took time to make a difference.

TODAY'S JOURNAL OF PERSONAL INSIGHTS

_____

_____

_____

_____

_____

_____

_____

_____

_____

_____

_____

_____

_____

"Young man, it's wonderful to be young! Enjoy every minute of it. Do everything you want to do; take it all in. But remember that you must give an account to God for everything you do" (Ecclesiastes 11:9).

MY SELF-EVALUATION—HOW WELL DID I DO TODAY?

You may grade yourself as you rate your day. This is between you and God.

❏ Praise, worship, and thanksgiving   ❏ Family time

❏ Prayer and extraordinary prayer   ❏ Time with friends

❏ Reading and meditating on the Word of God ❏ Reaching the lost

❏ Fasting and other sacrifices   ❏ Eating right and exercising

❏ Serving others in Christ-like love   ❏ Organizing myself to serve God

"So don't be troubled or afraid. Remember what I told you: I am going away, but I will come back to you again" (John 14:27-28).

Only 8 days to go in your *Countdown to Hope.*

SUSTAINING HOPE UNDER FIRE

"Yet I still dare to hope" (Lamentations 3:21).

When Jeremiah used the word "still" in Lamentations 3:21, he was speaking in defiance of something. He was under attack. He was being challenged. Something was trying to take away his reason for living. They were not only laughing at him. They also made up songs mocking him. He still had hope because he had steadfast trust in the future that was based on something real. It was not wishful thinking. It had substance.

Jeremiah was a prophet. He clung to the word he had received from God and stood on the basis of the veracity of God's Word. He was a vehicle of hope to people who were out of alignment with God.

If they had listened to him, if they had obeyed him, God could have backed the whole nation and things would have happened for their good and for His glory.

When Moses said to God, "Please, show me Your glory," God answered, "I will make all My goodness pass before you" (Exodus 33:18-19 NKJV). God wants to do good things in America that will do us good and give Him glory.

When the culture was out of alignment in Noah's day, God destroyed His creation but saved Noah and those with him in the ark. God was frustrated with His creation because what He had hoped for had not come to pass. The people He had created did not willfully submit to Him.

God creates people whom He expects to willfully choose to do what He says, not resist Him. He is all powerful. He could force us to obey Him, but He wants the creation itself to come into consensus with Him.

All sovereign spheres need to come into agreement with His will:

- *First in individuals submitting to His will for their lives*
- *Then in the family, church, and civil government*
- *Then voluntary associations in the spheres of education, art and entertainment, economics and finance*

Unless something is built on God, it has no enduring purpose. When these spheres come into alignment with God, people will find hope. They will find a reason for their existence that goes back to God. Everything in the future will come into alignment with the will of God.

THROUGH-THE-BIBLE IN ONE YEAR DAILY READING GUIDE

Fill in the four Bible chapters for today's date from the guide in the back of this journal.

Today's Four Bible Readings	My Personal Notes
☐ _____	_____
☐ _____	_____
☐ _____	_____
☐ _____	_____

MY PRAYER PRIORITIES FOR TODAY

My Right Relationship With God
_____
_____
_____

Leaders—Local, State, Nation, World
_____
_____
_____

Needs of Family and Friends
_____
_____
_____

Worldwide Revivals and Awakenings
_____
_____
_____

Five-Fold Ministry Church Leadership
_____
_____
_____

Praise and Thanksgiving
_____
_____
_____

REFUSING TO REMAIN SILENT WHEN TRUTH IS ATTACKED

"A dog barks when his master is attacked. I would be a coward if I saw that God's truth is attacked and yet would remain silent." —John Calvin (1509-1564)

MONEY MANAGEMENT AND WEALTH

"No eye has seen, no ear has heard, and no mind has imagined what God has prepared for those who love him" (1 Corinthians 2:9).

MY TREASURE CHEST OF HOPE

Counting My Many Blessings

Planning My Hopes and Dreams

GREAT TESTIMONIES OF HOPE—JOHN CALVIN

Persecuted preacher transformed society and still has influence today

One of the greatest influences on those who established America's system of government was John Calvin (1509-1564). This pastor's life gives us hope that America can be changed from a persecutor of the Church to its greatest advocate. Instead of removing prayer and the Bible from public life, leaders will call on pastors to restore America to God.

During colonial times, the Puritan John Winthrop's "city on a hill" principles for the Massachusetts Bay Colony followed Calvin's model of a system of civil government built on biblical truths. Every colonial charter referenced God and some, like Delaware, openly required civil authorities to be Christians. The checks and balances our founders wrote into their constitutions are based on concepts of man's sin nature that they learned about in the Church from the Bible and Calvin's principles.

Calvin was born in France but eventually fled his homeland when his association with Reformers who were opposed to the corrupt church structure came to the notice of the authorities. Eventually he would become one of the leading lights of the Reformers.

Although Calvin was born 500 years ago, his life and teachings still have a profound influence, and many Christians claim that a return to his principles is just what we need today. *What is often missed, however, is that Calvin spread his teachings by preaching, as the pastor of a church.* That is a challenge to pastors today—to have such a level of influence that what is preached in the pulpit is discussed and implemented by Congress.

In 1536 Calvin traveled to Geneva, Switzerland, for a one-day visit but was so well known that people prevailed on him to stay longer. Eventually in 1541 the Council of Geneva officially requested his return to Geneva and he remained there as a leading pastor in the city until he died in 1564. One man said after his death that "in this man there was exhibited to all an example of the life and death of the Christian, such as it will not be easy to depreciate, such as it will be difficult to emulate."

Reformers like Calvin constantly reaffirmed that the Scriptures were true and that the Bible was the only acceptable standard for human behavior. Their beliefs in those days could mean persecution or even death but they were led by the call of God. Driven out of England, France, and Scotland, they came for refuge to Geneva, which became the most important Protestant center of Europe. John Knox, mentioned earlier, a founder of the Presbyterian Church, came from Scotland to study under Calvin and became pastor of an English-speaking church.

It was said that men arrived as moderate Reformers and left as radical Calvinists who refused to allow the government to tell them what to do or to hinder them in any way from fulfilling the will of God. They didn't accept the myth that the Bible was suitable only for ceremonial occasions or private personal devotions. It applied to all of life.

Calvin imposed a strict moral code on Geneva based on the Bible. It transformed society. As in the book of Acts, deacons ministered to the poor. Pastors and teachers dealt with religious doctrines and disciplines.

As Christian pastors and leaders, we need to decide if we will give up and accept the suppression of our faith or if we will stand on the hope that if we become spiritual revolutionaries, America can be reformed.

We must call on God to give us the holy boldness of a Jeremiah and a John Calvin to declare that we will not bow down to sin and we will not compromise.

Unless we change course, God will surely judge America, but first He will begin by judging the church. We must dare to hope that preaching can bring transformation and that a civil government based on the Bible can bring restoration to every area of public life.

24-HOUR PERSONAL ACCOUNTABILITY JOURNAL
How I spent every hour of my life today

12 AM	
1 AM	
2 AM	
3 AM	
4 AM	
5 AM	
6 AM	
7 AM	
8 AM	
9 AM	
10 AM	
11 AM	
12 PM	
1 PM	
2 PM	
3 PM	
4 PM	
5 PM	
6 PM	
7 PM	
8 PM	
9 PM	
10 PM	
11 PM	

TODAY'S JOURNAL OF PERSONAL INSIGHTS

_____

_____

_____

_____

_____

_____

_____

_____

_____

_____

_____

"Yes, dear friends, we are already God's children, and we can't even imagine what we will be like when Christ returns. But we do know that when he comes we will be like him, for we will see him as he really is. And all who believe this will keep themselves pure, just as Christ is pure" (1 John 3:2-3).

MY SELF-EVALUATION—HOW WELL DID I DO TODAY?

You may grade yourself as you rate your day. This is between you and God.

❑ Praise, worship, and thanksgiving   ❑ Family time

❑ Prayer and extraordinary prayer   ❑ Time with friends

❑ Reading and meditating on the Word of God   ❑ Reaching the lost

❑ Fasting and other sacrifices   ❑ Eating right and exercising

❑ Serving others in Christ-like love   ❑ Organizing myself to serve God

"Look, the home of God is now among his people! He will live with them, and they will be his people. God himself will be with them. He will remove all of their sorrows, and there will be no more death or sorrow or crying or pain. For the old world and its evils are gone forever" (Revelation 21:3-4).

Only 7 days to go in your *Countdown to Hope.*

HOPING TO BE THE LIGHT OF THE WORLD

> " 'Do not be afraid, for I have ransomed you. I have called you
> by name; you are mine. When you go through deep waters and
> great trouble, I will be with you. When you go through rivers of
> difficulty, you will not drown! When you walk through the fire
> of oppression, you will not be burned up; the flames will not
> consume you. For I am the LORD, your God, the Holy One of
> Israel, your Savior' " (Isaiah 43:1-3).

When you have hope, you live in the daily expectation that your heart's desire will be fulfilled. We should be preparing as a church for the return of the God of glory Who says, "I will return for a glorious church." God hopes for a church in the future that has no spot or wrinkle nor any such thing (Ephesians 5:27). Right now the church in America has spots and wrinkles and every such thing.

In colonial America, communities required their civil leaders to be members in good standing in the church. They had to know God before they would know how to lead. It was the same in the Black community after slavery. We need to restore the churches as the light of the world.

How can a person who doesn't claim to have the Lord in the center of his life lead somebody who does? When a person who lives without God assumes leadership and diminishes the beliefs of those who know Jesus Christ, the children of disobedience are dominating the children of the light. Unbelievers may do some good, but God does not get the glory for it. The devil's children can do things that seem good but they don't lead you to God. They use the King's answers without the King.

We want people to come to Jesus and the devil wants the opposite. He is trying to ruin our country. God is using a remnant of faithful people to sustain America so that He does not have to judge and destroy it. We need a thickening on us that will impact the culture with the same intensity as Jonathan Edwards when he read in a monotone the manuscript "Sinners in the Hands of an Angry God." As mentioned earlier, that message was so powerful that people felt they couldn't hang on without falling into hell. It initiated the First Great Awakening of this country. It shook the nation. It was one man's manuscript read in a church but with God's backing it had the substance of hope in eternal reality.

Do you have this hope in you—Christ in you, the hope of glory (Colossians 1:27)? Somebody is supposed to have enough of God to shake a city and a nation. Is that you?

THROUGH-THE-BIBLE IN ONE YEAR DAILY READING GUIDE

Fill in the four Bible chapters for today's date from the guide in the back of this journal.

Today's Four Bible Readings	My Personal Notes
❑ _____	_____
❑ _____	_____
❑ _____	_____
❑ _____	_____

MY PRAYER PRIORITIES FOR TODAY

My Right Relationship With God

Leaders—Local, State, Nation, World

Needs of Family and Friends

Worldwide Revivals and Awakenings

Five-Fold Ministry Church Leadership

Praise and Thanksgiving

WORKING HARD WHILE RELYING ON CHRIST

*"We should so work as if we were to be saved by our works;
and so rely on Jesus Christ, as if we did no works."*
—Francis Asbury (1509-1564)

MONEY MANAGEMENT AND WEALTH

_____   _____
_____   _____
_____   _____
_____   _____

"For I am about to do a brand-new thing. See, I have already begun!
Do you not see it? I will make a pathway through the wilderness for
my people to come home" (Isaiah 43:19-20).

MY TREASURE CHEST OF HOPE

Counting My Many Blessings   Planning My Hopes and Dreams

_____   _____
_____   _____
_____   _____
_____   _____
_____   _____
_____   _____

GREAT TESTIMONIES OF HOPE—FRANCIS ASBURY

Saddleback circuit rider who changed American history

The spread of what we know as the Methodist Church in America
was led by Francis Asbury (1745-1816). He was saved in England as a
teenager and almost immediately began preaching. By age 26 he had
responded to John Wesley's call for preachers to go to America and 13
years later he was a national leader of the Methodist Episcopal movement.

Asbury preached to free and slave, Black and White. He was
outspoken against slavery. He ordained the first Black Methodist deacon,
Richard Allen, a former slave and the founder of the African Methodist
Episcopal Church. For 45 years, Asbury road an average of 6,000 miles a
year. He preached anywhere people would listen—open fields,
courthouses, tobacco houses, squares, and homes. In addition to preaching,
he had the ability to recruit, train, and organize circuit riders to cover the
mostly rural countryside with him.

*Many of the circuit riders had little formal education but
their personal conversions had been so dramatic that
they had a driving passion for winning others to Christ.*

The Methodist book of *Doctrines and Discipline* provided biblical principles from important Scripture texts. Pastors built their sermons and lesson plans for discipleship classes on that base. In spite of danger, fatigue, and sickness, through the efforts of Asbury and the other circuit riders the Methodists grew from 1,200 to 214,000 members in his lifetime. He ordained 700 preachers and founded several schools and colleges.

Church services were called "meetings." In addition to the meetings, the circuit riders or "saddlebag preachers" also taught Bible classes where they examined the members to determine what they were learning from Scripture. Sunday schools for children were organized where they were taught academic subjects in addition to learning the Bible.

FRANCIS ASBURY AND RICHARD ALLEN

1792. Richard Allen leaves St. George's Methodist Episcopal Church after disrespectful treatment by Whites who pulled him from his knees in church while he was praying to move him to another section.

1794. Allen founds Bethel Church in Philadelphia, later called "Mother Bethel." Begins meeting in former blacksmith shop.

1799. Bishop Francis Asbury ordains Allen as first Black deacon in Methodist Episcopal Church.

1805. Mother Bethel church building is completed.

1813. Congregation reaches 1,272 members.

1816. Asbury consecrates Allen as bishop of African Methodist Episcopal (AME) Church, independent denomination that Allen founded.

Today, the AME Church has more than two million members worldwide.

I have hope for the inner cities to be reached with the same zeal as Asbury reached the early colonies and Allen reached Black Americans. Do you have hope for any people group that desperately needs Jesus Christ? Would you have the dedication of a Francis Asbury, a Richard Allen, or a circuit rider to give your life on the basis of this hope?

24-HOUR PERSONAL ACCOUNTABILITY JOURNAL
How I spent every hour of my life today

12 AM	
1 AM	
2 AM	
3 AM	
4 AM	
5 AM	
6 AM	
7 AM	
8 AM	
9 AM	
10 AM	
11 AM	
12 PM	
1 PM	
2 PM	
3 PM	
4 PM	
5 PM	
6 PM	
7 PM	
8 PM	
9 PM	
10 PM	
11 PM	

TODAY'S JOURNAL OF PERSONAL INSIGHTS

_____

_____

_____

_____

_____

_____

_____

_____

_____

_____

_____

_____

_____

_____

"Plow up the hard ground of your hearts, for now is the time to seek the LORD, that he may come and shower righteousness upon you" (Hosea 10:12).

MY SELF-EVALUATION—HOW WELL DID I DO TODAY?

You may grade yourself as you rate your day. This is between you and God.

❏ Praise, worship, and thanksgiving   ❏ Family time

❏ Prayer and extraordinary prayer   ❏ Time with friends

❏ Reading and meditating on the Word of God   ❏ Reaching the lost

❏ Fasting and other sacrifices   ❏ Eating right and exercising

❏ Serving others in Christ-like love   ❏ Organizing myself to serve God

"Do not be like a senseless horse or mule that needs a bit and bridle to keep it under control. Many sorrows come to the wicked, but unfailing love surrounds those who trust the LORD" (Psalm 32:9-10).

Only 6 days to go in your *Countdown to Hope.*

ETERNAL VALUE OF HOPE

*"There are three things that will endure—faith, hope, and
love—and the greatest of these is love" (1 Corinthians 13:13).*

The Bible in 1 Corinthians 13 lists three eternal qualities that have been
mentioned throughout this journal—faith, hope, and love. They endure
because they come from God. Everything you do should be motivated by
love. Whatever you accomplish will happen by faith. Where you are going
is an issue of hope.

Hope gives you a reason for living. When your hope is built on
God's purpose for your life, it endures. It has enduring value. It never ends.

David Brainerd, the 17th century missionary to the Native
Americans you read about earlier, had faith that drove him to fulfill the
hope that he could reach them for Christ. He traveled on horseback through
storms, sickness, fatigue, and depression until he saw conversions.

Do you lack hope? Then get to know God and dedicate yourself to
a purpose higher than yourself and your comfort. Spend time with Him in
private devotion. Find out where God is taking you. Learn how to set daily
goals based on your hopes and dreams and according to the reality of
God's existence and His purpose for creating you.

Your most important goals are not determined by what *you* want.
If you want a good life full of hope you have to understand what *God*
wants. You can discover what He wants for you if you dedicate yourself to
prayer, reading and meditating on the Word of God, and examining your
life daily through this journal to see if you are following His plan.

God created you for a purpose—*His* purpose. You need to
discover that purpose. God hopes that your life will fulfill the purpose for
which He created you. When you understand that, His hope for you will
drive you on.

He created you to be a person of goals and vision, but to
accomplish your hopes and dreams alone is to be of all beings most
miserable. Goals and accomplishments are not enjoyed as an island. They
are enjoyed relationally.

When you fulfill God's will for your life within an ongoing
relationship with Him, you find true joy because you are pleasing someone
close to you. You dare to hope that your life is important to Him and that
what you do is necessary to help God accomplish His will in the earth.

THROUGH-THE-BIBLE IN ONE YEAR DAILY READING GUIDE

Fill in the four Bible chapters for today's date from the guide in the back of this journal.

Today's Four Bible Readings	My Personal Notes
❑ _____	_____
❑ _____	_____
❑ _____	_____
❑ _____	_____

MY PRAYER PRIORITIES FOR TODAY

My Right Relationship With God

_____
_____
_____

Leaders—Local, State, Nation, World

_____
_____
_____

Needs of Family and Friends

_____
_____
_____

Worldwide Revivals and Awakenings

_____
_____
_____

Five-Fold Ministry Church Leadership

_____
_____
_____

Praise and Thanksgiving

_____
_____
_____

INTENSE DESIRE TO BE ALONE WITH GOD

"I felt an intense desire to spend every moment for God. God is unspeakably gracious to me continually. In times past, he has given me inexpressible sweetness in the performance of duty. Frequently my soul has enjoyed much of God; but has been ready to say, 'Lord, it is good to be here.' "—David Brainerd (1718-1747)

MONEY MANAGEMENT AND WEALTH

_____   _____
_____   _____
_____   _____
_____   _____
_____   _____

" 'For I know the plans I have for you,' says the LORD. 'They are plans for good and not for disaster, to give you a future and a hope' " (Jeremiah 29:11).

MY TREASURE CHEST OF HOPE

Counting My Many Blessings   Planning My Hopes and Dreams

_____   _____
_____   _____
_____   _____
_____   _____
_____   _____
_____   _____
_____   _____

GREAT TESTIMONIES OF HOPE—DAVID BRAINERD

Trail of Tears becomes a Trail of Hope

In this era of modern hospitals, it is almost impossible to imagine bringing into your home a sick young man dying from tuberculosis, weak and spitting up blood, thus exposing your entire family to his disease. However, even today you might take that risk if you had the consecration of a Jonathan Edwards and the dying young man was David Brainerd.

By most standards, David Brainerd (1718-1747) seemed to be a failure in ministry for most of his life. As a young student at Yale, which was founded as a school to train Christian ministers and still functioned in that capacity in his day, Brainerd was converted to Christ in the midst of a controversy between "Old Lights"—professors who wanted to keep the Church as it was—and "New Lights"—those who were eager participants in America's First Great Awakening.

Brainerd privately criticized a Yale professor and someone reported it to the authorities. Since a rule had been passed forbidding criticism, it resulted in his humiliating expulsion, even though he was at the top of his class. Despite his repentance and requests for reinstatement, plus the intervention of Christian leaders, his expulsion stood. However, Brainerd's experience fueled the founding of other Christian colleges like Princeton that could accommodate the zeal of "New Lights."

David suffered greatly from sickness and frequent depressions, but he also had a genuine desire for intimacy with God and a driving sense of destiny. He spent days and weeks traveling the countryside—praying, searching his soul, and crying out to God for the salvation of Native Americans. He also kept an intimate spiritual diary. In August 1745, after years of keeping his hope alive, he was rewarded with a spiritual awakening among the Native Americans at Crossweeksung near Trenton, New Jersey. First his interpreter and his wife were saved, and then Native Americans came from miles around to hear him and were converted.

He established a Christian community and school for children and adults. The Lord gave him two more years to disciple them before he went to Edwards' home in Massachusetts to die.

> *In the two and a half centuries since Brainerd's death, his personal journal, edited by Jonathan Edwards, has inspired major Christian leaders like John Wesley and William Carey, who reached nations with the Gospel.*

In 1769, Eleazar Wheelock (a Congregationalist) read Brainerd's diary, went to the Iroquois and Algonquin tribes and founded a school to educate them that he later moved to Hanover, New Hampshire. *He named it "Dartmouth."*

In 1817, the American Board of Commissioners for Foreign Missions, an interdenominational outreach organized by Congregationalists, founded the Brainerd Mission. Many Cherokee were converted and built model communities, but in 1830 they were driven off their land by President Andrew Jackson. Thousands were forced to march to Oklahoma in the "Trail of Tears" where 4,000 died. However, Oklahoma descendants of the Cherokee people include the world-renowned Christian ministers *Oral Roberts and Kenneth Copeland.*

Only God knows how many people worldwide have found Christ and become dedicated disciples of Jesus through the tears of David Brainerd whose vital communion with God took him on a *Trail of Hope.*

24-HOUR PERSONAL ACCOUNTABILITY JOURNAL

How I spent every hour of my life today

12 AM	
1 AM	
2 AM	
3 AM	
4 AM	
5 AM	
6 AM	
7 AM	
8 AM	
9 AM	
10 AM	
11 AM	
12 PM	
1 PM	
2 PM	
3 PM	
4 PM	
5 PM	
6 PM	
7 PM	
8 PM	
9 PM	
10 PM	
11 PM	

TODAY'S JOURNAL OF PERSONAL INSIGHTS

_____
_____
_____
_____
_____
_____
_____
_____
_____
_____
_____
_____
_____
_____

"For if we would judge ourselves,
we should not be judged" (1 Corinthians 11:31 KJV).

MY SELF-EVALUATION—HOW WELL DID I DO TODAY?

You may grade yourself as you rate your day. This is between you and God.

❑ Praise, worship, and thanksgiving ❑ Family time

❑ Prayer and extraordinary prayer ❑ Time with friends

❑ Reading and meditating on the Word of God ❑ Reaching the lost

❑ Fasting and other sacrifices ❑ Eating right and exercising

❑ Serving others in Christ-like love ❑ Organizing myself to serve God

"But now we have confidence in a better hope,
through which we draw near to God" (Hebrews 7:19).

Only 5 days to go in your *Countdown to Hope.*

THE NEXT DIMENSION OF HOPE

*"God himself will be with them. He will remove all of their
sorrows, and there will be no more death or sorrow or crying
or pain. For the old world and its evils are gone forever"
(Revelation 21:3-4).*

Some day without warning God may unveil to you a dimension of the
spirit that you never thought of before. He will open the heavens and
you will find yourself looking forward to something that had never come to
your mind. You will enter into what the Bible calls "the new relationship
with God that comes by faith" (Romans 4:13).

That is the world you have been born for.

Inside of every born again believer are seeds of faith, hope, and
love. The Church passes down those enduring values generationally from
glory to glory, strength to strength, and faith to faith. Since two thousand
years have passed since Christ's resurrection, we should not be at the same
level as First Century Christians. We should be operating at a higher level.
It's quite obvious that we are not, but because we are people of hope the
Scripture can quicken that which is dead and call things that be not as
though they were. We can operate as people who think in terms of the
future and are building greater glory on the foundation of the past.

Paul had a revelation about hope and glory. He wrote in his letter
to the Colossians, "This message was kept secret for centuries and
generations past, but now it has been revealed to his own holy people. For
it has pleased God to tell his people that the riches and glory of Christ are
for you Gentiles, too. For this is the secret: Christ lives in you, and this is
your assurance that you will share in his glory" (Colossians 1:26-27).

That is powerful. God has actually given us His glory. Something
that has been hidden for centuries will be demonstrated through us and
give other people hope. An invisible force will be seen in a visible reality.

Angels can show up in an angelic display. God can give his angels
charge over us, to keep us in all our ways. But angels don't know joy.
There is something about your life that is an expression of joy in life itself.
The God of all hope wants you to have His hope as an abiding value.
Nothing that anyone can say to you can destroy or discourage you. You are
immune to criticism. You can hope without knowing what is going on
because you have been born again and supernaturally you receive an
infilling of hope and glory. The world needs someone like you.

Allow God to release His spirit of hope inside to take you to that
new dimension where you see clearly what you must do for God.

THROUGH-THE-BIBLE IN ONE YEAR DAILY READING GUIDE

Fill in the four Bible chapters for today's date from the guide in the back of this journal.

Today's Four Bible Readings	My Personal Notes
☐ _____	_____
☐ _____	_____
☐ _____	_____
☐ _____	_____

MY PRAYER PRIORITIES FOR TODAY

My Right Relationship With God

_____
_____
_____

Leaders—Local, State, Nation, World

_____
_____
_____

Needs of Family and Friends

_____
_____
_____

Worldwide Revivals and Awakenings

_____
_____
_____

Five-Fold Ministry Church Leadership

_____
_____
_____

Praise and Thanksgiving

_____
_____
_____

REGARDLESS OF SORROWS, IT IS WELL WITH MY SOUL

"When peace, like a river, attendeth my way,
When sorrows like sea-billows roll;
Whatever my lot, Thou hast taught me to say,
"It is well, it is well with my soul."
—Horatio G. Spafford (1828-1888) after his four daughters were lost at sea

MONEY MANAGEMENT AND WEALTH

_____   _____
_____   _____
_____   _____
_____   _____
_____   _____

". . . wisdom is sweet to your soul. If you find it, you will have a bright future, and your hopes will not be cut short" (Proverbs 24:14).

MY TREASURE CHEST OF HOPE

Counting My Many Blessings   Planning My Hopes and Dreams

_____   _____
_____   _____
_____   _____
_____   _____
_____   _____
_____   _____
_____   _____
_____   _____

GREAT TESTIMONIES OF HOPE—HORATIO SPAFFORD

In the midst of personal tragedy the hope that all is well

In the great Chicago fire of 1871 attorney Horatio G. Spafford and his family lost most of their wealth and personal property. Earlier they had lost their only son.

In 1874 his wife Anna and their four daughters left for England on the French ship *Villa de Havre*. As they approached the coast of Ireland, the ship collided with another ship and sank and 226 people died, including the Spaffords' four daughters.

Anna sent a terse cable to her husband, "saved alone."

Several weeks later, as he traveled to England to comfort his wife, he passed the place where the tragedy had occurred and God gave him a song that still encourages people today. He remembered Romans 8:28, "And we know that all things work together for good to them that love

God, to them who are the called according to his purpose" and wrote the words to "It Is Well with My Soul."

> *"When peace, like a river, attendeth my way,*
> *When sorrows like sea-billows roll;*
> *Whatever my lot, Thou hast taught me to say,*
> *'It is well, it is well with my soul.'*

> *"Though Satan should buffet, tho' trials should come,*
> *Let this blest assurance control,*
> *That Christ has regarded my helpless estate,*
> *And hath shed His own blood for my soul.*

> *"My sin—oh, the bliss of this glorious thought,*
> *My sin—not in part, but the whole,*
> *Is nailed to the cross and I bear it no more,*
> *Praise the Lord, praise the Lord, O my soul.*

> *"And, Lord haste the day when the faith shall be sight,*
> *The clouds be rolled back as a scroll,*
> *The trump shall resound and the Lord shall descend,*
> *'Even so'—it is well with my soul.*

> *"It is well with my soul,*
> *It is well, it is well with my soul."*

Throughout your life you are in the midst of an eternal battle of the soul against the spirit. The devil wants to keep you fleshly and hopeless, focused on your problems and trials. He wants to dash your hopes that God still cares for you regardless of how things look.

Sometimes tragic experiences like what happened to the Spaffords will seem so devastating that your soul—your mind, will, and emotions—fight against your hope. Take control until your soul is healed and well.

Reality is not remaining hopeless when times get hard. Reality is knowing that all things work together for good for those who love God.

24-HOUR PERSONAL ACCOUNTABILITY JOURNAL
How I spent every hour of my life today

12 AM	
1 AM	
2 AM	
3 AM	
4 AM	
5 AM	
6 AM	
7 AM	
8 AM	
9 AM	
10 AM	
11 AM	
12 PM	
1 PM	
2 PM	
3 PM	
4 PM	
5 PM	
6 PM	
7 PM	
8 PM	
9 PM	
10 PM	
11 PM	

TODAY'S JOURNAL OF PERSONAL INSIGHTS

_____

_____

_____

_____

_____

_____

_____

_____

_____

_____

_____

_____

_____

_____

"Who then will condemn us? Will Christ Jesus? No, for he is the one who died for us and was raised to life for us and is sitting at the place of highest honor next to God, pleading for us. Can anything ever separate us from Christ's love?" (Romans 8:34-35).

MY SELF-EVALUATION—HOW WELL DID I DO TODAY?

You may grade yourself as you rate your day. This is between you and God.

❑ Praise, worship, and thanksgiving   ❑ Family time

❑ Prayer and extraordinary prayer   ❑ Time with friends

❑ Reading and meditating on the Word of God   ❑ Reaching the lost

❑ Fasting and other sacrifices   ❑ Eating right and exercising

❑ Serving others in Christ-like love   ❑ Organizing myself to serve God

"And we know that God causes everything to work together for the good of those who love God and are called according to his purpose for them" (Romans 8:28).

Only 4 days to go in your *Countdown to Hope.*

EVER-INCREASING HOPE

*"Let the one who is doing wrong continue to do wrong; the one
who is vile, continue to be vile; the one who is good, continue
to do good; and the one who is holy, continue in holiness.
See, I am coming soon, and my reward is with me, to
repay all according to their deeds" (Revelation 22:11-12).*

R evelation 22 speaks of continuation and increase. Hope and goodness
are increasing in some people at the same time that vileness is
increasing in others. When there comes a decided parting of the waters
between good and evil, in the darkness of night you carry the light. You
don't have to float down a river that is dank and dirty. You can propel your
craft in a different direction. When you do, others will follow.

I don't believe that we will go to heaven alone. Everyone whose
life in God you have influenced will follow you. Everyone you helped to
leave behind the filthiness of the world will be there to greet you.

When everyone else is adrift, hope is the anchor of your soul
(Hebrews 6:18-19). You are not placing your hope in something
temporary. You are hoping in the unchanging nature of God and His Word.
He says, "I am the Lord. I change not." You trust Him in that declaration.

Trust, faith and hope work together. If you don't trust the Lord,
you don't have hope that He will come through for you and you don't
exercise your faith. However, if you hope in God you believe that what
you are hoping for will come to pass.

> *"O Lord, you alone are my hope.*
> *I've trusted you, O LORD, from childhood.*
> *Yes, you have been with me from birth;*
> *from my mother's womb you have cared for me.*
> *No wonder I am always praising you!*
> *My life is an example to many,*
> *because you have been my strength and protection"*
> *(Psalm 71:5-7).*

At some point in your Christian life a transformation occurs. You
not only have increasing hope in your thought-life but God Himself
becomes your hope. You are not just hoping that what He says will
happen. The reality of His existence in your life feeds your hope.

Love the Lord with all your heart. "Be of good courage,
And He shall strengthen your heart" (Psalm 27:14 NKJV).

THROUGH-THE-BIBLE IN ONE YEAR DAILY READING GUIDE

Fill in the four Bible chapters for today's date from the guide in the back of this journal.

Today's Four Bible Readings	My Personal Notes
☐ _____	_____
☐ _____	_____
☐ _____	_____
☐ _____	_____

MY PRAYER PRIORITIES FOR TODAY

My Right Relationship With God

_____
_____
_____

Leaders—Local, State, Nation, World

_____
_____
_____

Needs of Family and Friends

_____
_____
_____

Worldwide Revivals and Awakenings

_____
_____
_____

Five-Fold Ministry Church Leadership

_____
_____
_____

Praise and Thanksgiving

_____
_____
_____

MORE ALIVE THAN EVER IN ETERNITY

"Some day you will read in the papers that Moody is dead. Don't you believe a word of it. At that moment I shall be more alive than I am now. I was born of the flesh in 1837, I was born of the Spirit in 1855. That which is born of the flesh may die. That which is born of the Spirit shall live forever."—D.L. Moody (1837-1899)

MONEY MANAGEMENT AND WEALTH

_____   _____
_____   _____
_____   _____
_____   _____
_____   _____

*"So be strong and take courage, all you who put your hope in
the LORD!" (Psalm 31:24).*

MY TREASURE CHEST OF HOPE

Counting My Many Blessings   Planning My Hopes and Dreams

_____   _____
_____   _____
_____   _____
_____   _____
_____   _____
_____   _____
_____   _____
_____   _____

GREAT TESTIMONIES OF HOPE—D.L. MOODY

Finding hope after the Chicago fire

Dwight Lyman (D.L.) Moody (1837-1899) began his Christian
life with such little education that he could barely read the Bible aloud to
the children he won to Christ, but by the time he died he had left a Bible
institute, schools for children, and a worldwide evangelistic ministry still
changing lives today. His heart to win souls to Jesus at any cost produced
an enduring legacy.

He told a story to illustrate how he learned to walk in Jesus' steps:

*"There is a story of a Bohemian king, St. Wenceslas, going to
devotions in a distant church, one snowy winter night. His servant
followed, trying to imitate his zeal; but the way was rough, and he
began to faint. The king told him to step in the marks he made,
and he was able to follow. Christ commanded us to follow in His
steps. The path is smoother because He trod it."*

In the 19th century, Moody held huge crusades and reached continents for Christ, but he began by walking in Jesus' steps among the poor. His mission field was the ghetto and he made little provision for his own comfort. Instead of a home, he slept on a bench in a room at the Young Men's Christian Association (YMCA). There he prayed in secret in a coal closet under the stairs. His food was plain and he was able to stretch the contributions given to him by his friends to meet all of his expenses.

A turning point came in Moody's life after the Chicago fire of 1871 destroyed much of what he had worked for in ministry. After making sure that his children were safe, he and his wife worked tirelessly to help others. After losing so much that he had built up over the years, he realized that much of what he had accomplished had not been a result of a direct word from God but his own initiative. He made a commitment that in the future he would consult God first, not ask Him to bless the work later.

WORLDWIDE LEGACY OF D. L. MOODY (1837-1899)

- *Converted to Christ* as a teenager by his Sunday School teacher. Evangelist to children, eventually people of all ages. One million converts before he died.
- *Founded Colportage Association to produce literature* for "book missionaries" to spread the Gospel by giving away literature and then selling books door-to-door and through a book-of-the-month club (first of its kind).
- *Moody Press.* Colportage Association became Moody Press, which now provides literature for evangelism in 120 nations.
- *Moody Bible Institute and Moody Church.* Founded Chicago Evangelization Society in 1889, which was later renamed Moody Bible Institute. It was an outgrowth of the 1887 Chicago crusade. Founded a church in Chicago that was renamed Moody Church after his death.
- *Schools for boys and girls.* Founded Northfield Seminary (now Northfield School for Girls) in 1879, and the Mount Hermon School for Boys (1881) in Northfield, Massachusetts.
- *Revell Publishing.* Founded a newspaper for Sunday School materials, then convinced his brother-in-law, Fleming H. Revell, to take it over. It became a successful publishing company named after Revell.
- *Moody's first book*, a collection of sermons, sold 120,000 copies in the first year.
- *Million-seller song book.* He teamed with musician Ira Sankey to write a million-seller song book and donated all proceeds to charitable causes.

How much of your ministry came by a word from God and how much from your own initiative? As missionary C.T. Studd said, "Only one life, 'twill soon be past, Only what's done for Christ will last."

24-HOUR PERSONAL ACCOUNTABILITY JOURNAL
How I spent every hour of my life today

12 AM	
1 AM	
2 AM	
3 AM	
4 AM	
5 AM	
6 AM	
7 AM	
8 AM	
9 AM	
10 AM	
11 AM	
12 PM	
1 PM	
2 PM	
3 PM	
4 PM	
5 PM	
6 PM	
7 PM	
8 PM	
9 PM	
10 PM	
11 PM	

TODAY'S JOURNAL OF PERSONAL INSIGHTS

_____

_____

_____

_____

_____

_____

_____

_____

_____

_____

_____

"But I do nothing without consulting the Father. I judge as I am told. And my judgment is absolutely just, because it is according to the will of God who sent me; it is not merely my own" (John 5:30).

MY SELF-EVALUATION—HOW WELL DID I DO TODAY?

You may grade yourself as you rate your day. This is between you and God.

❑ Praise, worship, and thanksgiving   ❑ Family time

❑ Prayer and extraordinary prayer   ❑ Time with friends

❑ Reading and meditating on the Word of God   ❑ Reaching the lost

❑ Fasting and other sacrifices   ❑ Eating right and exercising

❑ Serving others in Christ-like love   ❑ Organizing myself to serve God

*"The nations of the earth will walk in its light,
and the rulers of the world will come and bring their glory to it.
Its gates never close at the end of day because there is no night. And all the nations
will bring their glory and honor into the city" (Revelation 21:24-26).*

Only 3 days to go in your *Countdown to Hope.*

THE SPLENDOR OF HOPE

"I cry out, 'My splendor is gone! Everything I had hoped for
from the LORD is lost!' The thought of my suffering and
homelessness is bitter beyond words. I will never forget this
awful time, as I grieve over my loss" (Lamentations 3:18-20).

When Jeremiah cried out, "My splendor is gone!" he had forgotten that he still had reasons to hope. He still had access to God because it was based on spiritual prosperity and relational equity, not on his circumstances.

When the Church, the Bride of Christ, comes down from God out of heaven (Revelation 21:2), she will be dressed in splendor. She will wear white linen, which is the righteousness of the saints (Revelation 19:8). The inner quality of righteousness will be manifested outwardly in the clothing of the saints.

We are accustomed to putting on coverings from the outside, but in the economy of God everything is grown from the inside. The splendor of righteousness grows from within and so does sin. When someone says, "I trust you," he is saying you have an inner trustworthiness. If he says, "You are lying to me," he is saying you have fallacies inside.

When your splendor is gone because of sin, the only way to restore it is repentance. You acknowledge your sin and repent and ask God to restore you because of the blood that Jesus shed for you.

The Bible says, "For God made Christ, who never sinned, to be the offering for our sin, so that we could be made right with God through Christ" (2 Corinthians 5:21). When Adam sinned, he felt naked before God. He lost his covering, which was his splendor. He had a covering of integrity because he was made in the image of God, but he lost it when he sinned. He should have said right away, "I was wrong," but he didn't do that. He blamed the woman, but God confronted him because he should have taken responsibility as the leader.

When God killed an animal and made coats of animal skins for Adam and his wife, that was the beginning of the blood line that extends from the Garden of Eden all the way to the last garden, Gethsemane, Golgotha and the cross.

When you lose your splendor, remember the cross and the blood Jesus shed for your sins. Then your hope and splendor will be restored.

THROUGH-THE-BIBLE IN ONE YEAR DAILY READING GUIDE

Fill in the four Bible chapters for today's date from the guide in the back of this journal.

Today's Four Bible Readings	My Personal Notes
☐ _____	_____
☐ _____	_____
☐ _____	_____
☐ _____	_____

MY PRAYER PRIORITIES FOR TODAY

My Right Relationship With God

_____
_____
_____

Leaders—Local, State, Nation, World

_____
_____
_____

Needs of Family and Friends

_____
_____
_____

Worldwide Revivals and Awakenings

_____
_____
_____

Five-Fold Ministry Church Leadership

_____
_____
_____

Praise and Thanksgiving

_____
_____
_____

STATE MUST GUARANTEE FREE EXPRESSION OF THE GOSPEL

*"The church is to promote holiness and thus to be the bulwark of the state.
The state in return is to give 'free passage' to the gospel."*
—Herbert L. Osgood, "The Political Ideas of the Puritans" (1891)

MONEY MANAGEMENT AND WEALTH

_____   _____
_____   _____
_____   _____
_____   _____
_____   _____

"For God is the one who provides seed for the farmer and then bread to eat. In the
same way, he will provide and increase your resources and then produce a great
harvest of generosity in you. Yes, you will be enriched in every way so that you can
always be generous" (2 Corinthians 9:10-11).

MY TREASURE CHEST OF HOPE

Counting My Many Blessings   Planning My Hopes and Dreams
_____   _____
_____   _____
_____   _____
_____   _____
_____   _____
_____   _____
_____   _____
_____   _____

GREAT TESTIMONIES OF HOPE—THE PURITANS

The Church as the foundation of the state

Black Americans of the 19th and early 20th century were
influenced by school teachers from the American Missionary Association
and other Christian organizations who had come from the North to educate
the freed slaves. Many teachers were descendants of the New England
Puritans, where in colonial times men could not qualify for state office
until they had demonstrated the reality of their faith to their churches.

Ministers in early America were the conscience of the state. Their
outspoken sermons and community activism kept elected officials in
alignment with the Bible. Politicians became qualified for office by
declaring that they believed in Jesus Christ as Lord and Savior and
accepted the Bible as truth. Elected officials had to sit in church every

Sunday while the pastor pounded into them the biblical principles by which they should make their decisions.

The following quote describes the church/state model used by the Puritans in colonial Massachusetts, patterned after John Calvin in Geneva. It also helps explain why Black pastors take such an active role in politics.

> *"The end of the state is to preserve 'external and temporal peace,' and that of the church to 'maintain internal and spiritual peace.' The work of both is to be done 'in all godliness and honesty.' Both are to be guided by the rules of the Word. The church is to promote holiness and thus to be the bulwark of the state. The state in return is to give 'free passage' to the gospel. ... Still, they have no authority to interfere in the election of church officers, to perform any ecclesiastical functions or to establish anything but a pure form of worship. Finally, all freemen should be church members, and magistrates should be chosen exclusively from them."*—Herbert L. Osgood, "The Political Ideas of the Puritans" (1891)

Here is a summary of the main points from the quote above:

- The Church maintains inner, spiritual peace. It promotes holiness, which gives stability to the state. It builds the character qualities necessary for individuals serving in state office.
- All candidates for office in the civil government must be church members.
- The state maintains peace in society. It provides protection for the freedom of the Church to spread the Gospel. It cannot interfere in church elections or functions.
- Leaders of both Church and state are expected to be godly and honest, guided by the Word of God.

Black Americans benefited greatly from the protection given to churches in America. Churches became places to develop spirituality and also character qualities of good citizens. Even though Blacks were rarely allowed to vote, run for office, or become social activists, when that opportunity came briefly during Reconstruction and later during the Civil Rights movement, the leadership training process was already in place in the Black church. Pastors like the Martin Luther King, Jr., Ralph Abernathy, and Fred Shuttlesworth were already established leaders.

The success of Black pastors in the Civil Rights movement as well as Puritan leaders from our past gives hope for a spiritual revival that will restore the Church as the foundation of the state in our day.

24-HOUR PERSONAL ACCOUNTABILITY JOURNAL
How I spent every hour of my life today

12 AM	
1 AM	
2 AM	
3 AM	
4 AM	
5 AM	
6 AM	
7 AM	
8 AM	
9 AM	
10 AM	
11 AM	
12 PM	
1 PM	
2 PM	
3 PM	
4 PM	
5 PM	
6 PM	
7 PM	
8 PM	
9 PM	
10 PM	
11 PM	

TODAY'S JOURNAL OF PERSONAL INSIGHTS

_____

_____

_____

_____

_____

_____

_____

_____

_____

_____

_____

_____

_____

_____

"So our aim is to please him always, whether we are here in this body or away from this body. For we must all stand before Christ to be judged. We will each receive whatever we deserve for the good or evil we have done in our bodies" (2 Corinthians 5:9-10).

MY SELF-EVALUATION—HOW WELL DID I DO TODAY?

You may grade yourself as you rate your day. This is between you and God.

❑ Praise, worship, and thanksgiving   ❑ Family time

❑ Prayer and extraordinary prayer   ❑ Time with friends

❑ Reading and meditating on the Word of God   ❑ Reaching the lost

❑ Fasting and other sacrifices   ❑ Eating right and exercising

❑ Serving others in Christ-like love   ❑ Organizing myself to serve God

"Doesn't your reverence for God give you confidence? Doesn't your life of integrity give you hope?" (Job 4:6).

Only 2 days to go in your *Countdown to Hope.*

HOPE OF ETERNAL LIFE

*"Then I saw a new heaven and a new earth, for the old heaven
and the old earth had disappeared. And the sea was also gone.
And I saw the holy city, the new Jerusalem, coming down from
God out of heaven like a beautiful bride prepared for her
husband" (Revelation 21:1-2).*

How do you wake up in the morning? Excited that it's a new day and
something good is about to happen? The Lord wants you to wake up
like a bride on her wedding day, thrilled about what lies ahead.

When you understand that you have a future as the bride of Christ,
the sun is always shining. It's easy to be positive. Hope fills your heart
because you know how much God values your life and you know you have
a destiny that He has ordained. God will keep you. He won't let you down.
He will fulfill His will in your life if you let Him.

Years ago when we were in Richmond we started an organization
called Foundation for the Future. God laid the foundation; therefore, the
future is our inheritance. What you learn about functioning in the kingdom
of God builds a sure foundation for a great future with Christ.

As a believer, you have a future on earth and a future in eternity.
Because of Adam's sin, you are born to die. You are restricted to a limited
number of years in this physical world, but when you are born again you
enter an unlimited dimension. The things that you learn every day about
marriage, administration, governing, or operating a business are not only
for this realm but also for eternity. You are learning how to operate like
God so that you can rule and reign with Him in eternity.

Can you imagine how it would misrepresent Christ if you whined
and complained or treated others with contempt? Could Jesus trust you to
oversee worlds? You can start now developing kinglike qualities. You are
already royalty. Carry yourself like a king and walk in hope.

When you wake up tomorrow, get excited about what you might
learn that you can take with you into the future because your future is
forever. Give God the first of all your increase at that precious time of the
day when you meet God. Let him feed you the substance of revelation. If
you don't know anything positive to say about yourself, just say what the
Lord says about you.

David said, "I will bless the LORD, who hath given me counsel"
(Psalm 16:7 KJV). Listen to the counsel of your trusted Friend.

THROUGH-THE-BIBLE IN ONE YEAR DAILY READING GUIDE

Fill in the four Bible chapters for today's date from the guide in the back of this journal.

Today's Four Bible Readings	My Personal Notes
☐ _____	_____
☐ _____	_____
☐ _____	_____
☐ _____	_____

MY PRAYER PRIORITIES FOR TODAY

My Right Relationship With God

_____
_____
_____
_____

Leaders—Local, State, Nation, World

_____
_____
_____
_____

Needs of Family and Friends

_____
_____
_____
_____

Worldwide Revivals and Awakenings

_____
_____
_____
_____

Five-Fold Ministry Church Leadership

_____
_____
_____
_____

Praise and Thanksgiving

_____
_____
_____
_____

NOT AFRAID TO BRING OTHERS TO CONVICTION OF SIN

"I see more than ever the need of making righteous people true in their inward parts. Let us be more thorough than ever with souls under conviction. Let us not be afraid to wound too deeply. Thousands of professors have never been truly convinced of sin, much less truly converted. Sin to them is being found out!"
—Catherine Booth (1703-1791)

MONEY MANAGEMENT AND WEALTH

_____   _____
_____   _____
_____   _____
_____   _____
_____   _____

.

"I wait for the LORD, my soul waits,
And in His word I do hope.
My soul waits for the Lord
More than those who watch for the morning"
(Psalm 130:5-6 NKJV).

MY TREASURE CHEST OF HOPE

Counting My Many Blessings   Planning My Hopes and Dreams
_____   _____
_____   _____
_____   _____
_____   _____
_____   _____
_____   _____
_____   _____
_____   _____

GREAT TESTIMONIES OF HOPE—CATHERINE BOOTH

Co-founder of Salvation Army enters next world with hope

As mentioned earlier, the Salvation Army was founded by William (1829-1912) and Catherine Booth (1829-1890). This husband and wife were such people of faith and so filled with the hope and vision of God that they could see the potential in people whom others called the worst dregs of society. Their lives were dedicated to others' salvation.

One day Catherine received word from her doctor that she had terminal cancer. She went home and told her husband. He said later, "I was stunned. I felt as if the whole world were coming to a standstill. Opposite me, on the wall, was a picture of Christ on the cross. I thought I could understand it then, as never before. She talked to me like an angel; she talked as she had never talked before. I could say little or nothing. I could only kneel with her and try to pray."

During the final months of her life, she tried to continue her work as long as she was able, until finally weakness forced her to be confined to her bed. Delegations of Salvation Army recruits came to hear her words of wisdom and witness her incredible peace as she waited to pass on.

Catherine Booth died at the age of 61 after a lifetime of dedication to others for the cause of Christ. As she passed, she was full of hope, fearless, and ready for the next world she knew so well. She said:

> *"My dear children and Friends, I have loved you so much, and in God's strength have helped you a little. Now, at His call, I am going away from you. The War must go on. Self-Denial will prove your love to Christ. All must do something. I send you my blessing. Fight on, and God be with you. Victory comes at last. I will meet you in Heaven."*

Her son Bramwell Booth wrote of his mother's passing:

> *"Soon after noon, I felt the deepening darkness of the long valley of the shadows was closing around my dear mother, and a little later I took my last farewell. Her lips moved, and she gave me one look of inexpressible tenderness and trust, which will live with me for ever. Again we sang:*

> *" 'My mistakes His free grace doth cover,*
> *My sins He doth wash away;*
> *These feet which shrink and falter*
> *Shall enter the Gates of Day.' "*

Her family had seen her dedication to her family, her Lord, other Christians, and sinners who were lost. She served each day as if it could be her last, and one day it was.

You prepare for heaven by creating the environment of Heaven in your heart. You have private fellowship with God. You grow in the character of Christ, preparing to be His Bride. You submit to authority and stay in fellowship with a local church (the Salvation Army is a church). As you read through this book, you write in your journal about God's Word and document how you spend your time each day.

When Catherine Booth died, everything in her life had been written in a book in heaven. Imagine her rewards when she met the Lord and He said, "Well done, my good and faithful servant" (Matthew 25:21).

24-HOUR PERSONAL ACCOUNTABILITY JOURNAL

How I spent every hour of my life today

12 AM	
1 AM	
2 AM	
3 AM	
4 AM	
5 AM	
6 AM	
7 AM	
8 AM	
9 AM	
10 AM	
11 AM	
12 PM	
1 PM	
2 PM	
3 PM	
4 PM	
5 PM	
6 PM	
7 PM	
8 PM	
9 PM	
10 PM	
11 PM	

TODAY'S JOURNAL OF PERSONAL INSIGHTS

_____

_____

_____

_____

_____

_____

_____

_____

_____

_____

_____

_____

_____

"Put me on trial, LORD, and cross-examine me. Test my motives and affections.
For I am constantly aware of your unfailing love, and
I have lived according to your truth" (Psalm 26:2-3).

MY SELF-EVALUATION—HOW WELL DID I DO TODAY?

You may grade yourself as you rate your day. This is between you and God.

❑ Praise, worship, and thanksgiving   ❑ Family time

❑ Prayer and extraordinary prayer   ❑ Time with friends

❑ Reading and meditating on the Word of God   ❑ Reaching the lost

❑ Fasting and other sacrifices   ❑ Eating right and exercising

❑ Serving others in Christ-like love   ❑ Organizing myself to serve God

"The LORD is my light and my salvation; whom shall I fear? the LORD is the
strength of my life; of whom shall I be afraid?" (Psalm 27:1 KJV).

Only 1 day to go in your *Countdown to Hope.*

HOPE OF A KINGDOM UNDER CHRIST

*"The kingdoms of this world are become the kingdoms of our
Lord, and of his Christ; and he shall reign for ever and ever"
(Revelation 11:15 KJV).*

Before the world began, God knew how it would end. Then He worked backwards to make it a reality. Revelation speaks of the end-times hope of the church that all kingdoms will one day come under Christ.

Jesus told the apostles that in the world to come they would be assigned responsibilities in His kingdom. He said, "You have remained true to me in my time of trial. And just as my Father has granted me a Kingdom, I now grant you the right to eat and drink at my table in that Kingdom. And you will sit on thrones. judging the twelve tribes of Israel" (Luke 22:28-30). That appointment follows creative order. God delegated certain responsibilities over the earth to Adam—animals, birds, creeping things and fish. Jesus will delegate certain responsibilities over eternity to His Church. At every moment, we are in on-the-job training for the future.

When you cultivate humility, service, and a repentant heart, you walk in hope that God will promote you to a position of greatness, both in this world and the world to come. He says, "I live in a high and holy place, but also with him who is contrite and lowly in spirit, to revive the spirit of the lowly and to revive the heart of the contrite" (Isaiah 57:15 KJV).

Each stage in life is preparation for the next level of responsibility. This life is a preparation for the life to come. God has prepared a whole new experience for those who love Him. That's why you need to get all you can get out of God's training program on earth because that is what He is using to qualify you to rule with Christ in eternity.

Everything about God is eternal. However, the hope for eternity that God has placed inside of you is constantly being choked off by "the cares of this world, and the deceitfulness of riches, and the lusts of other things" (Mark 4:19). Remember—no matter what problems arise, no matter how hard life seems to get, no matter what tragedies and pains you have to endure, it's not the end. There is always hope.

You are on a journey of hope without end, and when you know the Lord every place you go is even more awesome than the place you were before. God wants you to live in the eternal realm. The Bible, prayer, personal accountability, faithfulness to your family, submission to authority in a church, leadership in the marketplace from a biblical perspective—all these things keep bringing you back to God's reality until the end comes and God's vision for you and for all the earth is fulfilled.

THROUGH-THE-BIBLE IN ONE YEAR DAILY READING GUIDE

Fill in the four Bible chapters for today's date from the guide in the back of this journal.

Today's Four Bible Readings	My Personal Notes
☐ _____	_____
☐ _____	_____
☐ _____	_____
☐ _____	_____

MY PRAYER PRIORITIES FOR TODAY

My Right Relationship With God

_____
_____
_____
_____

Leaders—Local, State, Nation, World

_____
_____
_____
_____

Needs of Family and Friends

_____
_____
_____
_____

Worldwide Revivals and Awakenings

_____
_____
_____
_____

Five-Fold Ministry Church Leadership

_____
_____
_____
_____

Praise and Thanksgiving

_____
_____
_____
_____

SPIRIT OF THE LORD WITHSTANDS THE FLOOD

"The death toll climbed relentlessly, but inside the dark, damp chapel survivors sang praises to the Lord. . . . 'We don't understand the meaning of it all or the purpose of it. But we feel very strongly that God is in control,' said A. J. Moser, vice president and dean of the college." —Atlanta Journal article on Toccoa Falls flood

"When the enemy shall come in like a flood, the Spirit of the LORD shall lift up a standard against him."—Isaiah 59:19 KJV

MONEY MANAGEMENT AND WEALTH

_____   _____
_____   _____
_____   _____
_____   _____

"And he sought God in the days of Zechariah, who had understanding in the
visions of God: and as long as he sought the LORD, God made him to prosper"
(2 Chronicles 26:5).

MY TREASURE CHEST OF HOPE

Counting My Many Blessings   Planning My Hopes and Dreams

_____   _____
_____   _____
_____   _____
_____   _____
_____   _____
_____   _____
_____   _____
_____   _____

GREAT TESTIMONIES OF HOPE—TOCCOA FALLS FLOOD

A sudden flood sweeps people into eternity but hope remains

The deluge sounded like a freight train roaring out of the darkness
in the early morning hours of November 7, 1977. Then came the shouts.
"The dam has broken!" A gentle waterfall tumbling over Georgia's
forested Toccoa Falls had become a deadly 30-foot-high wall of water as
the dam broke after heavy rain and released a 40-acre lake above.

The flood bolted over the falls and crashed into the valley below
smashing trailers, homes, and educational buildings on the campus of
Toccoa Falls College, an evangelical Christian school associated with the
Christian and Missionary Alliance. Trees were uprooted like match sticks.
Cars and house trailers became deadly torpedoes.

People struggled to escape. Some were swept away. Others
watched helplessly as members of their own family drowned before their

eyes. The families and the school would never be the same. In a flash, 39 men, women, and children were sent into eternity.

As the waters receded, incredible stories began to emerge out of Georgia's worst natural disaster in almost 40 years. A community of professing Christians had come face to face with the reality of their belief in eternal life and the world was watching to see what they would do.

The Bible says, "Many waters cannot quench love, neither can the floods drown it" (Song of Solomon 8:7 KJV). They lost loved ones, but the love of Jesus could not be drowned. Even members of the press and rescue agencies who came to see what remained of the campus could not believe that the survivors had such peace and joy. They had not lost hope because they knew their loved ones were with Jesus. They did not stay bound to the realm of their earthly circumstances. They moved into the realm of the eternal. All of their lives had been a preparation for this hour.

In one trailer, Bill and Karen Anderson had been asleep with their five children when a woman ran by shouting, *"The dam has broken!"* Within seconds, a huge force slammed against the trailer, tearing off the roof. They cried out to God to help them not to panic and managed to calm their children by telling them to trust the Lord.

When the next blow came the children cried out, *"Jesus! Jesus!"* The trailer smashed against trees. Bill tossed his oldest daughter, 12, and oldest son, 6, into the branches. Then he heard his wife saying calmly to two of the other children in the hallway of the trailer, "Come on, kids, get ready. We're going to meet Jesus." And then they were washed away. Bill knew they were with the Lord.

Bill and his other daughter managed to survive, along with the two children in the trees. When Bill's unsaved relatives came for the funeral, he discovered that this seeming tragedy had a victorious side.

His sister told him, "I've found the Lord."

His oldest brother said, "I didn't come here for the funeral. . . . I'm here to see you. I want what you've got," and Bill led him to the Savior.

Bill knew where his wife and children were, and now he knew that his brother and sister would be with them some day in the future. The deaths had already transcended the realm of time and brought the reality of eternity to the earth.

24-HOUR PERSONAL ACCOUNTABILITY JOURNAL

How I spent every hour of my life today

12 AM	
1 AM	
2 AM	
3 AM	
4 AM	
5 AM	
6 AM	
7 AM	
8 AM	
9 AM	
10 AM	
11 AM	
12 PM	
1 PM	
2 PM	
3 PM	
4 PM	
5 PM	
6 PM	
7 PM	
8 PM	
9 PM	
10 PM	
11 PM	

TODAY'S JOURNAL OF PERSONAL INSIGHTS

_____

_____

_____

_____

_____

_____

_____

_____

_____

_____

_____

_____

_____

"I will show you what it's like when someone comes to me, listens to my teaching, and then obeys me. It is like a person who builds a house on a strong foundation laid upon the underlying rock. When the floodwaters rise and break against the house, it stands firm because it is well built" (Luke 6:47-48).

MY SELF-EVALUATION—HOW WELL DID I DO TODAY?

You may grade yourself as you rate your day. This is between you and God.

❑ Praise, worship, and thanksgiving   ❑ Family time

❑ Prayer and extraordinary prayer   ❑ Time with friends

❑ Reading and meditating on the Word of God   ❑ Reaching the lost

❑ Fasting and other sacrifices   ❑ Eating right and exercising

❑ Serving others in Christ-like love   ❑ Organizing myself to serve God

"Great is his faithfulness; his mercies begin afresh each day. I say to myself, 'The LORD is my inheritance; therefore, I will hope in him!' " (Lamentations 3:23-24).

Your *Countdown to Hope* is ended. Go in peace into your new way of life.

WHERE WILL YOU GO FROM HERE?

You have just read in the final day of your Countdown to Hope that each stage in life is preparation for the next. This life is a preparation for the life to come. You need to get all you can get out of God's training program on earth because that is what He is using to qualify you to rule with Christ in eternity.

How can you get more out of God's training program in your *Dare to Hope* journal? After 30 days of documenting your activities and building your hopes and dreams, it would be good to reflect on what you have discovered and then decide on your hope focus for the days ahead. You can use the next pages to write notes and chart your future course.

- Do you understand more fully your calling and future hope?
- Do you have a new commitment to maintaining a hopeful attitude?
- Are you more disciplined regarding how you spend each day?
- Are you more dedicated to prayer and reading of the Word?

Continuing your journey on www.daretohopejournal.com

Now that you have taken this journey with me, I want to provide you with more opportunities to grow in Christ-like character. You will find more resources on our journal website, www.daretohopejournal.com.

I look forward to continuing this journey with you. See you there!

What I have learned and where I want to go from here . . .

What I have learned and where I want to go from here . . .

_____

_____

_____

_____

_____

_____

_____

_____

_____

_____

_____

_____

_____

_____

_____

_____

_____

_____

_____

_____

_____

Section 3

Through-the-Bible
Reading Guide

SPECIAL NOTE: *Although this is a dated reading guide, not everyone will be able to start this guide on January 1. Whenever you begin, simply find that date and start there. In that way, all of us will be reading the same chapters of the Bible together on the same days of the year. At the end of the year, keep reading until you have completed the entire Bible in one year.*

Read One Chapter from Four Sections of the Bible Every Day. Complete the Entire Bible in One Year.

Eight divisions of the Bible used in the reading guide:

Pentateuch. Genesis, Exodus, Leviticus, Numbers, Deuteronomy

History. Joshua, Judges, Ruth, 1 Samuel, 2 Samuel, 1 Kings, 2 Kings, Ezra, Nehemiah, Esther *(1 and 2 Chronicles are read at the end of the Epistles)*

Poetry. Job, Psalms, Song of Solomon *(Ecclesiastes is read at the end of the Prophet)*

Wisdom. Proverbs *(repeated during the year)*

Prophets. Jeremiah, Lamentations, Ezekiel, Hosea, Joel, Amos, Obadiah, Jonah, Micah, Nahum, Habakkuk, Zephaniah, Haggai, Zechariah, Malachi *(Isaiah is read after the Gospels and Acts.)*

Gospels. Matthew, Mark, Luke, John *(followed by Acts and Isaiah.*

Epistles. Romans, 1 Corinthians, 2 Corinthians, Galatians, Ephesians, Philippians, Colossians, 1 Thessalonians, 2 Thessalonians, 1 Timothy, 2 Timothy, Titus, Philemon, Hebrews, James, 1 Peter, 2 Peter, 1 John, 2 John, 3 John, Jude *(followed by 1 and 2 Chronicles)*

End Times. Daniel, Revelation *(repeated during the year)*

January

This month as you read Genesis 12 and 13, notice the Lord's call upon Abram (Abraham), the man we now call a patriarch. The Lord identified Himself with Abraham's earthly lineage when He said, "I am the God of Abraham, Isaac and Jacob." Those were people whom He called out of darkness. They didn't have the light of His reality until God made Himself known to them. That is true for every one of us. The Bible says that we grope at noonday. We know by nature that God *exists* but we don't know God *personally* unless He reveals Himself to us. Abram didn't have a Bible to read, so God changed him until his life became the Bible that we read. As you seek to know Jesus Christ through the Word and prayer, live in such a way that when people read your life, it fills their hearts with faith.

Jan 1	❑Gen 1	❑Josh 1	❑Job 1	❑Prv 1
Jan 2	❑Gen 2	❑Josh 2	❑Job 2	❑Prv 2
Jan 3	❑Gen 3	❑Josh 3	❑Job 3	❑Prv 3
Jan 4	❑Gen 4	❑Josh 4	❑Job 4	❑Prv 4
Jan 5	❑Gen 5	❑Josh 5	❑Job 5	❑Prv 5
Jan 6	❑Gen 6	❑Josh 6	❑Job 6	❑Prv 6
Jan 7	❑Gen 7	❑Josh 7	❑Job 7	❑Prv 7
Jan 8	❑Jer 1	❑Matt 1	❑Rom 1	❑Dan 1
Jan 9	❑Jer 2	❑Matt 2	❑Rom 2	❑Dan 2
Jan 10	❑Jer 3	❑Matt 3	❑Rom 3	❑Dan 3
Jan 11	❑Jer 4	❑Matt 4	❑Rom 4	❑Dan 4
Jan 12	❑Jer 5	❑Matt 5	❑Rom 5	❑Dan 5
Jan 13	❑Jer 6	❑Matt 6	❑Rom 6	❑Dan 6
Jan 14	❑Jer 7	❑Matt 7	❑Rom 7	❑Dan 7
Jan 15	❑Gen 8	❑Josh 8	❑Job 8	❑Prv 8
Jan 16	❑Gen 9	❑Josh 9	❑Job 9	❑Prv 9
Jan 17	❑Gen 10	❑Josh 10	❑Job 10	❑Prv 10
Jan 18	❑Gen 11	❑Josh 11	❑Job 11	❑Prv 11
Jan 19	❑Gen 12	❑Josh 12	❑Job 12	❑Prv 12
Jan 20	❑Gen 13	❑Josh 13	❑Job 13	❑Prv 13
Jan 21	❑Gen 14	❑Josh 14	❑Job 14	❑Prv 14
Jan 22	❑Jer 8	❑Matt 8	❑Rom 8	❑Dan 8
Jan 23	❑Jer 9	❑Matt 9	❑Rom 9	❑Dan 9
Jan 24	❑Jer 10	❑Matt 10	❑Rom 10	❑Dan 10
Jan 25	❑Jer 11	❑Matt 11	❑Rom 11	❑Dan 11
Jan 26	❑Jer 12	❑Matt 12	❑Rom 12	❑Dan 12
Jan 27	❑Jer 13	❑Matt 13	❑Rom 13	❑Rev 1
Jan 28	❑Jer 14	❑Matt 14	❑Rom 14	❑Rev 2
Jan 29	❑Gen 15	❑Josh 15	❑Job 15	❑Prv 15
Jan 30	❑Gen 16	❑Josh 16	❑Job 16	❑Prv 16
Jan 31	❑Gen 17	❑Josh 17	❑Job 17	❑Prv 17

February

During Black History Month, we would do well to remember that because of their history, the people of Black America have the potential to be both spiritually and naturally the strongest Christian missionaries that the world has ever seen. As people of color, they can cross international boundaries and speak freely of their faith. They have favor throughout the earth. Statistically, Black America is dying. In almost every category—abortion, disease, family breakdown, murder, imprisonment—they have the worst statistics among all of the people groups in our country. In the inner cities, many have abandoned hope. They have lost their sense of destiny. They need preachers like you to bring them to Jesus, and then they will take the Gospel to the nations. They may be a mission field now, but some day they will be missionaries to the world.

Feb 1	❑Gen 18	❑Josh 18	❑Job 18	❑Prv 18
Feb 2	❑Gen 19	❑Josh 19	❑Job 19	❑Prv 19
Feb 3	❑Gen 20	❑Josh 20	❑Job 20	❑Prv 20
Feb 4	❑Gen 21	❑Josh 21	❑Job 21	❑Prv 21
Feb 5	❑Jer 15	❑Matt 15	❑Rom 15	❑Rev 3
Feb 6	❑Jer 16	❑Matt 16	❑Rom 16	❑Rev 4
Feb 7	❑Jer 17	❑Matt 17	❑1 Cor 1	❑Rev 5
Feb 8	❑Jer 18	❑Matt 18	❑1 Cor 2	❑Rev 6
Feb 9	❑Jer 19	❑Matt 19	❑1 Cor 3	❑Rev 7
Feb 10	❑Jer 20	❑Matt 20	❑1 Cor 4	❑Rev 8
Feb 11	❑Jer 21	❑Matt 21	❑1 Cor 5	❑Rev 9
Feb 12	❑Gen 22	❑Josh 22	❑Job 22	❑Prv 22
Feb 13	❑Gen 23	❑Josh 23	❑Job 23	❑Prv 23
Feb 14	❑Gen 24	❑Josh 24	❑Job 24	❑Prv 24
Feb 15	❑Gen 25	❑Judg 1	❑Job 25	❑Prv 25
Feb 16	❑Gen 26	❑Judg 2	❑Job 26	❑Prv 26
Feb 17	❑Gen 27	❑Judg 3	❑Job 27	❑Prv 27
Feb 18	❑Gen 28	❑Judg 4	❑Job 28	❑Prv 28
Feb 19	❑Jer 22	❑Matt 22	❑1 Cor 6	❑Rev 10
Feb 20	❑Jer 23	❑Matt 23	❑1 Cor 7	❑Rev 11
Feb 21	❑Jer 24	❑Matt 24	❑1 Cor 8	❑Rev 12
Feb 22	❑Jer 25	❑Matt 25	❑1 Cor 9	❑Rev 13
Feb 23	❑Jer 26	❑Matt 26	❑1 Cor 10	❑Rev 14
Feb 24	❑Jer 27	❑Matt 27	❑1 Cor 11	❑Rev 15
Feb 25	❑Jer 28	❑Matt 28	❑1 Cor 12	❑Rev 16
Feb 26	❑Gen 29	❑Judg 5	❑Job 29	❑Prv 29
Feb 27	❑Gen 30	❑Judg 6	❑Job 30	❑Prv 30
Feb 28	❑Gen 31	❑Judg 7	❑Job 31	❑Prv 31

March

God is raising up a people whom the world has never seen before. They have a sense of destiny. They don't live for themselves. They have been kept by God. Like Job, the devil's attacks against them have failed because the Lord has something awesome in store for them to do. Ask God to give you a sense of brokenness like the awakening that came on Job after his trials. Where you have resisted God and the conviction of the Holy Spirit, break down and repent, because that is when times of refreshing will come. Acknowledge God's greatness and commit yourself to His ways. You are not called to carry guilt and condemnation. You are called to walk in the peace that passes understanding that comes from a surrendered life. When you receive an impartation and quickening from the Holy Ghost, say "Yes" to God.

Mar 1	❏Gen 32	❏Judg 8	❏Job 32	❏Prv 1
Mar 2	❏Gen 33	❏Judg 9	❏Job 33	❏Prv 2
Mar 3	❏Gen 34	❏Judg 10	❏Job 34	❏Prv 3
Mar 4	❏Gen 35	❏Judg 11	❏Job 35	❏Prv 4
Mar 5	❏Jer 29	❏Mark 1	❏1 Cor 13	❏Rev 17
Mar 6	❏Jer 30	❏Mark 2	❏1 Cor 14	❏Rev 18
Mar 7	❏Jer 31	❏Mark 3	❏1 Cor 15	❏Rev 19
Mar 8	❏Jer 32	❏Mark 4	❏1 Cor 16	❏Rev 20
Mar 9	❏Jer 33	❏Mark 5	❏2 Cor 1	❏Rev 21
Mar 10	❏Jer 34	❏Mark 6	❏2 Cor 2	❏Rev 22
Mar 11	❏Jer 35	❏Mark 7	❏2 Cor 3	❏Dan 1
Mar 12	❏Gen 36	❏Judg 12	❏Job 36	❏Prv 5
Mar 13	❏Gen 37	❏Judg 13	❏Job 37	❏Prv 6
Mar 14	❏Gen 38	❏Judg 14	❏Job 38	❏Prv 7
Mar 15	❏Gen 39	❏Judg 15	❏Job 39	❏Prv 8
Mar 16	❏Gen 40	❏Judg 16	❏Job 40	❏Prv 9
Mar 17	❏Gen 41	❏Judg 17	❏Job 41	❏Prv 10
Mar 18	❏Gen 42	❏Judg 18	❏Job 42	❏Prv 11
Mar 19	❏Jer 36	❏Mark 8	❏2 Cor 4	❏Dan 2
Mar 20	❏Jer 37	❏Mark 9	❏2 Cor 5	❏Dan 3
Mar 21	❏Jer 38	❏Mark 10	❏2 Cor 6	❏Dan 4
Mar 22	❏Jer 39	❏Mark 11	❏2 Cor 7	❏Dan 5
Mar 23	❏Jer 40	❏Mark 12	❏2 Cor 8	❏Dan 6
Mar 24	❏Jer 41	❏Mark 13	❏2 Cor 9	❏Dan 7
Mar 25	❏Jer 42	❏Mark 14	❏2 Cor 10	❏Dan 8
Mar 26	❏Gen 43	❏Judg 19	❏Ps 1	❏Prv 12
Mar 27	❏Gen 44	❏Judg 20	❏Ps 2	❏Prv 13
Mar 28	❏Gen 45	❏Judg 21	❏Ps 3	❏Prv 14
Mar 29	❏Gen 46	❏Ruth 1	❏Ps 4	❏Prv 15
Mar 30	❏Gen 47	❏Ruth 2	❏Ps 5	❏Prv 16
Mar 31	❏Gen 48	❏Ruth 3	❏Ps 6	❏Prv 17

April

This month as you read about Jesus' death, burial, and resurrection, remember God's mercy. Even though man fell, God made a way for us to be restored to Him. The only Person who could meet the perfect standard of God was Jesus Christ. God said that the soul who sins shall surely die. That means He has a right to kill every one of us right now, but He made a way so that we would not be destroyed. His mercy is not a license to sin. His mercy gives you time to recognize your weaknesses, rededicate yourself to God, and become more serious for God today than you were yesterday. God has never changed His mind about His calling on your life. Even when you change your mind, God has not changed His mind. His grace is on you right now. The Lord sees you beyond how you see yourself.

Apr 1	❏Gen 49	❏Ruth 4	❏Ps 7	❏Prv 18
Apr 2	❏Jer 43	❏Mark 15	❏2 Cor 11	❏Dan 9
Apr 3	❏Jer 44	❏Mark 16	❏2 Cor 12	❏Dan 10
Apr 4	❏Jer 45	❏Luke 1	❏2 Cor 13	❏Dan 11
Apr 5	❏Jer 46	❏Luke 2	❏Gal 1	❏Dan 12
Apr 6	❏Jer 47	❏Luke 3	❏Gal 2	❏Rev 1
Apr 7	❏Jer 48	❏Luke 4	❏Gal 3	❏Rev 2
Apr 8	❏Jer 49	❏Luke 5	❏Gal 4	❏Rev 3
Apr 9	❏Gen 50	❏1 Sam 1	❏Ps 8	❏Prv 19
Apr 10	❏Ex 1	❏1 Sam 2	❏Ps 9	❏Prv 20
Apr 11	❏Ex 2	❏1 Sam 3	❏Ps 10	❏Prv 21
Apr 12	❏Ex 3	❏1 Sam 4	❏Ps 11	❏Prv 22
Apr 13	❏Ex 4	❏1 Sam 5	❏Ps 12	❏Prv 23
Apr 14	❏Ex 5	❏1 Sam 6	❏Ps 13	❏Prv 24
Apr 15	❏Ex 6	❏1 Sam 7	❏Ps 14	❏Prv 25
Apr 16	❏Jer 50	❏Luke 6	❏Gal 5	❏Rev 4
Apr 17	❏Jer 51	❏Luke 7	❏Gal 6	❏Rev 5
Apr 18	❏Jer 52	❏Luke 8	❏Eph 1	❏Rev 6
Apr 19	❏Lam 1	❏Luke 9	❏Eph 2	❏Rev 7
Apr 20	❏Lam 2	❏Luke 10	❏Eph 3	❏Rev 8
Apr 21	❏Lam 3	❏Luke 11	❏Eph 4	❏Rev 9
Apr 22	❏Lam 4	❏Luke 12	❏Eph 5	❏Rev 10
Apr 23	❏Ex 7	❏1 Sam 8	❏Ps 15	❏Prv 26
Apr 24	❏Ex 8	❏1 Sam 9	❏Ps 16	❏Prv 27
Apr 25	❏Ex 9	❏1 Sam 10	❏Ps 17	❏Prv 28
Apr 26	❏Ex 10	❏1 Sam 11	❏Ps 18	❏Prv 29
Apr 27	❏Ex 11	❏1 Sam 12	❏Ps 19	❏Prv 30
Apr 28	❏Ex 12	❏1 Sam 13	❏Ps 20	❏Prv 31
Apr 29	❏Ex 13	❏1 Sam 14	❏Ps 21	❏Prv 1
Apr 30	❏Lam 5	❏Luke 13	❏Eph 6	❏Rev 11

May

In Exodus 20 you will read again the Ten Commandments that include God's command to honor your father and mother. He promised that when you do so you will enjoy a good long life. On Mother's Day, remember to honor your mother. Remember also Mary, the mother of Jesus, who submitted herself to a word from God so that seed could be conceived in a willing vessel. Whatever God wants to impart to you, receive it and allow it to grow to fullness so that He can accomplish His will in the earth through you.

May 1	❑Ezek 1	❑Luke 14	❑Php 1	❑Rev 12
May 2	❑Ezek 2	❑Luke 15	❑Php 2	❑Rev 13
May 3	❑Ezek 3	❑Luke 16	❑Php 3	❑Rev 14
May 4	❑Ezek 4	❑Luke 17	❑Php 4	❑Rev 15
May 5	❑Ezek 5	❑Luke 18	❑Col 1	❑Rev 16
May 6	❑Ezek 6	❑Luke 19	❑Col 2	❑Rev 17
May 7	❑Ex 14	❑1 Sam 15	❑Ps 22	❑Prv 2
May 8	❑Ex 15	❑1 Sam 16	❑Ps 23	❑Prv 3
May 9	❑Ex 16	❑1 Sam 17	❑Ps 24	❑Prv 4
May 10	❑Ex 17	❑1 Sam 18	❑Ps 25	❑Prv 5
May 11	❑Ex 18	❑1 Sam 19	❑Ps 26	❑Prv 6
May 12	❑Ex 19	❑1 Sam 20	❑Ps 27	❑Prv 7
May 13	❑Ex 20	❑1 Sam 21	❑Ps 28	❑Prv 8
May 14	❑Ezek 7	❑Luke 20	❑Col 3	❑Rev 18
May 15	❑Ezek 8	❑Luke 21	❑Col 4	❑Rev 19
May 16	❑Ezek 9	❑Luke 22	❑1 Ths 1	❑Rev 20
May 17	❑Ezek 10	❑Luke 23	❑1 Ths 2	❑Rev 21
May 18	❑Ezek 11	❑Luke 24	❑1 Ths 3	❑Rev 22
May 19	❑Ezek 12	❑John 1	❑1 Ths 4	❑Dan 1
May 20	❑Ezek 13	❑John 2	❑1 Ths 5	❑Dan 2
May 21	❑Ex 21	❑1 Sam 22	❑Ps 29	❑Prv 9
May 22	❑Ex 22	❑1 Sam 23	❑Ps 30	❑Prv 10
May 23	❑Ex 23	❑1 Sam 24	❑Ps 31	❑Prv 11
May 24	❑Ex 24	❑1 Sam 25	❑Ps 32	❑Prv 12
May 25	❑Ex 25	❑1 Sam 26	❑Ps 33	❑Prv 13
May 26	❑Ex 26	❑1 Sam 27	❑Ps 34	❑Prv 14
May 27	❑Ex 27	❑1 Sam 28	❑Ps 35	❑Prv 15
May 28	❑Ezek 14	❑John 3	❑2 Ths 1	❑Dan 3
May 29	❑Ezek 15	❑John 4	❑2 Ths 2	❑Dan 4
May 30	❑Ezek 16	❑John 5	❑2 Ths 3	❑Dan 5
May 31	❑Ezek 17	❑John 6	❑1 Tim 1	❑Dan 6

June

One of the greatest things any Christian can do is to raise up spiritual children after you—sons and daughters who look like you in the spirit and follow you as you follow Christ. Daniel 11:32 says that "the people who know their God will be strong and do exploits." On Father's Day, honor your natural father and remember that you are becoming spiritually strong so that you can do great things for God, including carrying others as a spiritual father, regardless of your gender. Bring sinners to birth in prayer until they are born again.

Jun 1	❑Ezek 18	❑John 7	❑1 Tim 2	❑Dan 7
Jun 2	❑Ezek 19	❑John 8	❑1 Tim 3	❑Dan 8
Jun 3	❑Ezek 20	❑John 9	❑1 Tim 4	❑Dan 9
Jun 4	❑Ex 28	❑1 Sam 29	❑Ps 36	❑Prv 16
Jun 5	❑Ex 29	❑1 Sam 30	❑Ps 37	❑Prv 17
Jun 6	❑Ex 30	❑1 Sam 31	❑Ps 38	❑Prv 18
Jun 7	❑Ex 31	❑2 Sam 1	❑Ps 39	❑Prv 19
Jun 8	❑Ex 32	❑2 Sam 2	❑Ps 40	❑Prv 20
Jun 9	❑Ex 33	❑2 Sam 3	❑Ps 41	❑Prv 21
Jun 10	❑Ex 34	❑2 Sam 4	❑Ps 42	❑Prv 22
Jun 11	❑Ezek 21	❑John 10	❑1 Tim 5	❑Dan 10
Jun 12	❑Ezek 22	❑John 11	❑1 Tim 6	❑Dan 11
Jun 13	❑Ezek 23	❑John 12	❑2 Tim 1	❑Dan 12
Jun 14	❑Ezek 24	❑John 13	❑2 Tim 2	❑Rev 1
Jun 15	❑Ezek 25	❑John 14	❑2 Tim 3	❑Rev 2
Jun 16	❑Ezek 26	❑John 15	❑2 Tim 4	❑Rev 3
Jun 17	❑Ezek 27	❑John 16	❑Titus 1	❑Rev 4
Jun 18	❑Ex 35	❑2 Sam 5	❑Ps 43	❑Prv 23
Jun 19	❑Ex 36	❑2 Sam 6	❑Ps 44	❑Prv 24
Jun 20	❑Ex 37	❑2 Sam 7	❑Ps 45	❑Prv 25
Jun 21	❑Ex 38	❑2 Sam 8	❑Ps 46	❑Prv 26
Jun 22	❑Ex 39	❑2 Sam 9	❑Ps 47	❑Prv 27
Jun 23	❑Ex 40	❑2 Sam 10	❑Ps 48	❑Prv 28
Jun 24	❑Lev 1	❑2 Sam 11	❑Ps 49	❑Prv 29
Jun 25	❑Ezek 28	❑John 17	❑Titus 2	❑Rev 5
Jun 26	❑Ezek 29	❑John 18	❑Titus 3	❑Rev 6
Jun 27	❑Ezek 30	❑John 19	❑Phile 1	❑Rev 7
Jun 28	❑Ezek 31	❑John 20	❑Heb 1	❑Rev 8
Jun 29	❑Ezek 32	❑John 21	❑Heb 2	❑Rev 9
Jun 30	❑Ezek 33	❑Acts 1	❑Heb 3	❑Rev 10

July

As you celebrate Independence Day this month, remember that the most influential people in the founding of America were those who started with the Bible and a relationship with God through Jesus Christ as the basis for both Church and state. A government "of the people" meant the people in covenant with God and one another, bound by His laws and committed to seeing God's Law enforced through the laws of the land. Social institutions in America—including colleges, hospitals, and work among the poor—were established on the foundation of the Bible. There was no "separation of church and state," because they understood that only godly people were fit to govern.

"Every person who shall be chosen a member of either house, or appointed to any office or place of trust, before taking his seat, or entering upon the execution of his office, shall take the following oath, or affirmation . . . 'I, A.B. do profess faith in God the Father, and in Jesus Christ His only Son, and in the Holy Ghost, one God, blessed for evermore; and I do acknowledge the holy scriptures of the Old and New Testament to be given by divine inspiration."

Constitution of Delaware, 1776

Jul 1	❑Ezek 34	❑Acts 2	❑Heb 4	❑Rev 11
Jul 2	❑Lev 2	❑2 Sam 12	❑Ps 50	❑Prv 30
Jul 3	❑Lev 3	❑2 Sam 13	❑Ps 51	❑Prv 31
Jul 4	❑Lev 4	❑2 Sam 14	❑Ps 52	❑Prv 1
Jul 5	❑Lev 5	❑2 Sam 15	❑Ps 53	❑Prv 2
Jul 6	❑Lev 6	❑2 Sam 16	❑Ps 54	❑Prv 3
Jul 7	❑Lev 7	❑2 Sam 17	❑Ps 55	❑Prv 4
Jul 8	❑Lev 8	❑2 Sam 18	❑Ps 56	❑Prv 5
Jul 9	❑Ezek 35	❑Acts 3	❑Heb 5	❑Rev 12
Jul 10	❑Ezek 36	❑Acts 4	❑Heb 6	❑Rev 13
Jul 11	❑Ezek 37	❑Acts 5	❑Heb 7	❑Rev 14
Jul 12	❑Ezek 38	❑Acts 6	❑Heb 8	❑Rev 15
Jul 13	❑Ezek 39	❑Acts 7	❑Heb 9	❑Rev 16
Jul 14	❑Ezek 40	❑Acts 8	❑Heb 10	❑Rev 17
Jul 15	❑Ezel 41	❑Acts 9	❑Heb 11	❑Rev 18
Jul 16	❑Lev 9	❑2 Sam 19	❑Ps 57	❑Prv 6
Jul 17	❑Lev 10	❑2 Sam 20	❑Ps 58	❑Prv 7
Jul 18	❑Lev 11	❑2 Sam 21	❑Ps 59	❑Prv 8
Jul 19	❑Lev 12	❑2 Sam 22	❑Ps 60	❑Prv 9
Jul 20	❑Lev 13	❑2 Sam 23	❑Ps 61	❑Prv 10
Jul 21	❑Lev 14	❑2 Sam 24	❑Ps 62	❑Prv 11
Jul 22	❑Lev 15	❑1 Kng 1	❑Ps 63	❑Prv 12
Jul 23	❑Ezek 42	❑Acts 10	❑Heb 12	❑Rev 19
Jul 24	❑Ezek 43	❑Acts 11	❑Heb 13	❑Rev 20
Jul 25	❑Ezek 44	❑Acts 12	❑James 1	❑Rev 21
Jul 26	❑Ezek 45	❑Acts 13	❑James 2	❑Rev 22
Jul 27	❑Ezek 46	❑Acts 14	❑James 3	❑Dan 1
Jul 28	❑Ezek 47	❑Acts 15	❑James 4	❑Dan 2
Jul 29	❑Ezek 48	❑Acts 16	❑James 5	❑Dan 3
Jul 30	❑Lev 16	❑1 Kng 2	❑Ps 64	❑Prv 13
Jul 31	❑Lev 17	❑1 Kng 3	❑Ps 65	❑Prv 14

August

None of us can keep the Law as described in Leviticus, but God made a way for us to find favor with Him by following our Lord and Savior, Jesus Christ, "who Himself bore our sins in His own body on the tree, that we, having died to sins, might live for righteousness—by whose stripes you were healed" (1 Peter 2:24 NKJV). With His stripes, we can receive spiritual healing from our past and be reconciled to God and one another. We can receive physical healing and be empowered to fulfill His will.

Aug 1	❑Lev 18	❑1 Kng 4	❑Ps 66	❑Prv 15
Aug 2	❑Lev 19	❑1 Kng 5	❑Ps 67	❑Prv 16
Aug 3	❑Lev 20	❑1 Kng 6	❑Ps 68	❑Prv 17
Aug 4	❑Lev 21	❑1 Kng 7	❑Ps 69	❑Prv 18
Aug 5	❑Lev 22	❑1 Kng 8	❑Ps 70	❑Prv 19
Aug 6	❑Hosea 1	❑Acts 17	❑1 Pet 1	❑Dan 4
Aug 7	❑Hosea 2	❑Acts 18	❑1 Pet 2	❑Dan 5
Aug 8	❑Hosea 3	❑Acts 19	❑1 Pet 3	❑Dan 6
Aug 9	❑Hosea 4	❑Acts 20	❑1 Pet 4	❑Dan 7
Aug 10	❑Hosea 5	❑Acts 21	❑1 Pet 5	❑Dan 8
Aug 11	❑Hosea 6	❑Acts 22	❑2 Pet 1	❑Dan 9
Aug 12	❑Hosea 7	❑Acts 23	❑2 Pet 2	❑Dan 10
Aug 13	❑Lev 23	❑1 Kng 9	❑Ps 71	❑Prv 20
Aug 14	❑Lev 24	❑1 Kng 10	❑Ps 72	❑Prv 21
Aug 15	❑Lev 25	❑1 Kng 11	❑Ps 73	❑Prv 22
Aug 16	❑Lev 26	❑1 Kng 12	❑Ps 74	❑Prv 23
Aug 17	❑Lev 27	❑1 Kng 13	❑Ps 75	❑Prv 24
Aug 18	❑Num 1	❑1 Kng 14	❑Ps 76	❑Prv 25
Aug 19	❑Num 2	❑1 Kng 15	❑Ps 77	❑Prv 26
Aug 20	❑Hosea 8	❑Acts 24	❑2 Pet 3	❑Dan 11
Aug 21	❑Hosea 9	❑Acts 25	❑1 John 1	❑Dan 12
Aug 22	❑Hosea 10	❑Acts 26	❑1 John 2	❑Rev 1
Aug 23	❑Hosea 11	❑Acts 27	❑1 John 3	❑Rev 2
Aug 24	❑Hosea 12	❑Acts 28	❑1 John 4	❑Rev 3
Aug 25	❑Hosea 13	❑Isa 1	❑1 John 5	❑Rev 4
Aug 26	❑Hosea 14	❑Isa 2	❑2 John 1	❑Rev 5
Aug 27	❑Num 3	❑1 Kng 16	❑Ps 78	❑Prv 27
Aug 28	❑Num 4	❑1 Kng 17	❑Ps 79	❑Prv 28
Aug 29	❑Num 5	❑1 Kng 18	❑Ps 80	❑Prv 29
Aug 30	❑Num 6	❑1 Kng 19	❑Ps 81	❑Prv 30
Aug 31	❑Num 7	❑1 Kng 20	❑Ps 82	❑Prv 31

September

This month you will read in Numbers 13 how all the spies but Joshua and Caleb saw themselves as grasshoppers compared to the inhabitants of the land. That was because they had a grasshopper mentality. The giants felt that they could beat them because the children of Israel saw themselves small. You can't solve social issues with a small mind. You need the mind of Christ. You can't do anything with crime when you think you can't. You can't reconcile racial divisions if you think it is too hard. Jesus is in you. The Word is in you. The Holy Ghost is with you. The blood of Jesus covers you. Jesus isn't coming here and seeing terrorism and challenging social issues and saying, "I can't do anything. It is too much for Me to handle." Jesus isn't backing off anything. In Christ there are no chumps. You are anointed. God has nobody else to work with but you. You're the one.

Sep 1	❏Num 8	❏1 Kng 21	❏Ps 83	❏Prv 1
Sep 2	❏Num 9	❏1 Kng 22	❏Ps 84	❏Prv 2
Sep 3	❏Joel 1	❏Isa 3	❏3 John 1	❏Rev 6
Sep 4	❏Joel 2	❏Isa 4	❏Jude	❏Rev 7
Sep 5	❏Joel 3	❏Isa 5	❏1 Chr 1	❏Rev 8
Sep 6	❏Amos 1	❏Isa 6	❏1 Chr 2	❏Rev 9
Sep 7	❏Amos 2	❏Isa 7	❏1 Chr 3	❏Rev 10
Sep 8	❏Amos 3	❏Isaah 8	❏1 Chr 4	❏Rev 11
Sep 9	❏Amos 4	❏Isa 9	❏1 Chr 5	❏Rev 12
Sep 10	❏Num 10	❏2 Kng 1	❏Ps 85	❏Prv 3
Sep 11	❏Num 11	❏2 Kng 2	❏Ps 86	❏Prv 4
Sep 12	❏Num 12	❏2 Kng 3	❏Ps 87	❏Prv 5
Sep 13	❏Num 13	❏2 Kng 4	❏Ps 88	❏Prv 6
Sep 14	❏Num 14	❏2 Kng 5	❏Ps 89	❏Prv 7
Sep 15	❏Num 15	❏2 Kng 6	❏Ps 90	❏Prv 8
Sep 16	❏Num 16	❏2 Kng 7	❏Ps 91	❏Prv 9
Sep 17	❏Amos 5	❏Isa 10	❏1 Chr 6	❏Rev 13
Sep 18	❏Amos 6	❏Isa 11	❏1 Chr 7	❏Rev 14
Sep 19	❏Amos 7	❏Isa 12	❏1 Chr 8	❏Rev 15
Sep 20	❏Amos 8	❏Isa 13	❏1 Chr 9	❏Rev 16
Sep 21	❏Amos 9	❏Isa 14	❏1 Chr 10	❏Rev 17
Sep 22	❏Obad 1	❏Isa 15	❏1 Chr 11	❏Rev 18
Sep 23	❏Jon 1	❏Isa 16	❏1 Chr 12	❏Rev 19
Sep 24	❏Num 17	❏2 Kng 8	❏Ps 92-93	❏Prv 10
Sep 25	❏Num 18	❏2 Kng 9	❏Ps 94-95	❏Prv 11
Sep 26	❏Num 19	❏2 Kng 10	❏Ps 96-97	❏Prv 12
Sep 27	❏Num 20	❏2 Kng 11	❏Ps 98-99	❏Prv 13
Sep 28	❏Num 21	❏2 Kng 12	❏Ps 100-101	❏Prv 14
Sep 29	❏Num 22	❏2 Kng 13	❏Ps 102	❏Prv 15
Sep 30	❏Num 23	❏2 Kng 14	❏Ps 103	❏Prv 16

October

In Proverbs 29:2 you will read, "When the godly are in authority, the people rejoice. But when the wicked are in power, they groan." America has a destiny from God that requires godly leaders. Christians live for the life to come. Every aspect of our lives prepares us for the future when time is no more. In the next world, you will have delegated responsibilities. You will receive rewards, but you are being qualified by the way you live and govern now. John Winthrop, an early governor of the Massachusetts Bay Colony, knew the destiny of America. He said in 1630, "We shall find that the God of Israel is among us, when ten of us shall be able to resist a thousand of our enemies; when He shall make us a praise and glory that men shall say of succeeding plantations, 'may the Lord make it like that of New England.' For we must consider that we shall be as a city upon a hill. The eyes of all people are upon us."

Oct 1	❑Jon 2	❑Isa 17	❑1 Chr 13	❑Rev 20
Oct 2	❑Jon 3	❑Isa 18	❑1 Chr 14	❑Rev 21
Oct 3	❑Jon 4	❑Isa 19	❑1 Chr 15	❑Rev 22
Oct 4	❑Micah 1	❑Isa 20	❑1 Chr 16	❑Dan 1
Oct 5	❑Micah 2	❑Isa 21	❑1 Chr 17	❑Dan 2
Oct 6	❑Micah 3	❑Isa 22	❑1 Chr 18	❑Dan 3
Oct 7	❑Micah 4	❑Isa 23	❑1 Chr 19	❑Dan 4
Oct 8	❑Num 24	❑2 Kng 15	❑Ps 104	❑Prv 17
Oct 9	❑Num 25	❑2 Kng 16	❑Ps 105	❑Prv 18
Oct 10	❑Num 26	❑2 Kng 17	❑Ps 106	❑Prv 19
Oct 11	❑Num 27	❑2 Kng 18	❑Ps 107	❑Prv 20
Oct 12	❑Num 28	❑2 Kng 19	❑Ps 108-109	❑Prv 21
Oct 13	❑Num 29	❑2 Kng 20	❑Ps 110-111	❑Prv 22
Oct 14	❑Num 30	❑2 Kng 21	❑Ps 112-113	❑Prv 23
Oct 15	❑Micah 5	❑Isa 24	❑1Chr 20-21	❑Dan 5
Oct 16	❑Micah 6	❑Isa 25	❑1 Chr 22	❑Dan 6
Oct 17	❑Micah 7	❑Isa 26	❑1 Chr 23	❑Dan 7
Oct 18	❑Nah 1	❑Isa 27	❑1Chr 24-25	❑Dan 8
Oct 19	❑Nah 2	❑Isa 28	❑1 Chr 26	❑Dan 9
Oct 20	❑Nah 3	❑Isa 29	❑1 Chr 27	❑Dan 10
Oct 21	❑Hab 1	❑Isa 30	❑1 Chr 28	❑Dan 11
Oct 22	❑Num 31	❑2 Kng 22	❑Ps 114-115	❑Prv 24
Oct 23	❑Num 32	❑2 Kng 23	❑Ps 116-117	❑Prv 25
Oct 24	❑Num 33	❑2 Kng 24	❑Ps 118	❑Prv 26
Oct 25	❑Num 34	❑2 Kng 25	❑Ps 119	❑Prv 27
Oct 26	❑Num 35	❑Ezra 1	❑Ps 120-121	❑Prv 28
Oct 27	❑Num 36	❑Ezra 2	❑Ps 122-123	❑Prv 29
Oct 28	❑Deut 1	❑Ezra 3	❑Ps 124-125	❑Prv 30
Oct 29	❑Hab 2	❑Isa 31	❑1 Chr 29	❑Dan 12
Oct 30	❑Hab 3	❑Isa 32	❑2 Chr 1	❑Rev 1
Oct 31	❑Zeph 1	❑Isa 33	❑2 Chr 2	❑Rev 2

November

Remember as you read Psalm 133 this month that the Church is called to be unified. The body of Christ is not just a group of individuals. It is a new man, including Blacks, Whites, Asians, Arabs, Hispanics—every race of people on earth. All of us are the body of Christ if Jesus has come into our hearts. No part of the body can say that it has no need of the other part. The eye can't say to the ear, "I have no need of you." The leg can't say to the feet, "I have no need of you." Every part of the body is important. (See 1 Corinthians 12-14.) Psalm 133 says, "Behold how good and pleasant it is for brethren to dwell together in unity. It is like the precious ointment upon the head."

Nov 1	❑Zeph 2	❑Isa 34	❑2 Chr 3	❑Rev 3
Nov 2	❑Zeph 3	❑Isa 35	❑2 Chr 4	❑Rev 4
Nov 3	❑Hagg 1	❑Isa 36	❑2 Chr 5	❑Rev 5
Nov 4	❑Hagg 2	❑Isa 37	❑2 Chr 6	❑Rev 6
Nov 5	❑Deut 2	❑Ezra 4	❑Ps 126-127	❑Prv 31
Nov 6	❑Deut 3	❑Ezra 5	❑Ps 128-129	❑Prv 1
Nov 7	❑Deut 4	❑Ezra 6	❑Ps 130-131	❑Prv 2
Nov 8	❑Deut 5	❑Ezra 7	❑Ps 132-133	❑Prv 3
Nov 9	❑Deut 6	❑Ezra 8	❑Ps 134-135	❑Prv 4
Nov 10	❑Deut 7	❑Ezra 9	❑Ps 136	❑Prv 5
Nov 11	❑Deut 8	❑Ezra 10	❑Ps 137	❑Prv 6
Nov 12	❑Zech 1	❑Isa 38	❑2 Chr 7	❑Rev 7
Nov 13	❑Zech 2	❑Isa 39	❑2 Chr 8	❑Rev 8
Nov 14	❑Zech 3	❑Isa 40	❑2 Chr 9	❑Rev 9
Nov 15	❑Zech 4	❑Isa 41	❑2Chr 10-11	❑Rev 10
Nov 16	❑Zech 5	❑Isa 42	❑2Chr 12-13	❑Rev 11
Nov 17	❑Zech 6	❑Isa 43	❑2 Chr 14	❑Rev 12
Nov 18	❑Zech 7	❑Isa 44	❑2 Chr 15	❑Rev 13
Nov 19	❑Deut 9	❑Neh 1	❑Ps 138	❑Prv 7
Nov 20	❑Deut 10	❑Neh 2	❑Ps 139	❑Prv 8
Nov 21	❑Deut 11	❑Neh 3	❑Ps 140	❑Prv 9
Nov 22	❑Deut 12	❑Neh 4	❑Ps 141	❑Prv 10
Nov 23	❑Deut 13	❑Neh 5	❑Ps 142	❑Prv 11
Nov 24	❑Deut 14	❑Neh 6	❑Ps 143	❑Prv 12
Nov 25	❑Deut 15	❑Neh 7	❑Ps 144	❑Prv 13
Nov 26	❑Zech 8	❑Isa 45	❑2 Chr 16	❑Rev 14
Nov 27	❑Zech 9	❑Isa 46	❑2 Chr 17	❑Rev 15
Nov 28	❑Zech 10	❑Isa 47	❑2 Chr 18	❑Rev 16
Nov 29	❑Zech 11-12	❑Isa 48	❑2 Chr 19	❑Rev 17
Nov 30	❑Zech 13-14	❑Isa 49	❑2 Chr 20	❑Rev 18

December

Jesus, Emmanuel, God with us, has come! It's time to wake up and run to the inner cities and all the other dark places of the earth! Arise and shine! Light has come to you in the Person of Jesus Christ. Take His light to the darkness, and you will find treasures there—treasures of darkness—that only show up to those who carry His light.

> "Arise, shine; for your light has come! And the glory of the LORD is risen upon you. For behold, the darkness shall cover the earth, and deep darkness the people; but the LORD will arise over you, and His glory will be seen upon you. The Gentiles shall come to your light, and kings to the brightness of your rising" (Isaiah 60:1-3 NKJV).

Dec 1	❏Mal 1	❏Isa 50	❏2 Chr 21	❏Rev 19
Dec 2	❏Mal 2	❏Isa 51	❏2 Chr 22	❏Rev 20
Dec 3	❏Deut 16	❏Neh 8	❏Ps 145	❏Prv 7
Dec 4	❏Deut 17	❏Neh 9-10	❏Ps 146	❏Prv 8
Dec 5	❏Deut 18	❏Neh 11-12	❏Ps 147	❏Prv 9
Dec 6	❏Deut 19	❏Neh 13	❏Ps 148	❏Prv 10
Dec 7	❏Deut 20	❏Est 1	❏Ps 149	❏Prv 11
Dec 8	❏Deut 21	❏Est 2	❏Ps 150	❏Prv 12
Dec 9	❏Deut 22	❏Est 3	❏Song 1	❏Prv 13
Dec 10	❏Mal 3	❏Isa 52	❏2 Chr 23	❏Rev 21
Dec 11	❏Mal 4	❏Isa 53	❏2 Chr 24	❏Rev 22
Dec 12	❏Eccl 1	❏Isa 54	❏2 Chr 25	❏Dan 1
Dec 13	❏Eccl 2	❏Isa 55	❏2 Chr 26	❏Dan 2
Dec 14	❏Eccl 3	❏Isa 56-57	❏2 Chr 27	❏Dan 3
Dec 15	❏Eccl 4	❏Isa 58	❏2 Chr 28	❏Dan 4
Dec 16	❏Eccl 5	❏Isa 59	❏2 Chr 29	❏Dan 5
Dec 17	❏Deut 23-24	❏Est 4	❏Song 2	❏Prv 7
Dec 18	❏Deut 25-26	❏Est 5	❏Song 3	❏Prv 8
Dec 19	❏Deut 27	❏Est 6	❏Song 4	❏Prv 9
Dec 20	❏Deut 28	❏Est 7	❏Song 5	❏Prv 10
Dec 21	❏Deut 29-30	❏Est 8	❏Song 6	❏Prv 11
Dec 22	❏Deut 31-32	❏Est 9	❏Song 7	❏Prv 12
Dec 23	❏Deut 33-34	❏Est 10	❏Song 8	❏Prv 13
Dec 24	❏Eccl 6	❏Isa 60	❏2 Chr 30	❏Dan 6
Dec 25	❏Eccl 7	❏Isa 61	❏2 Chr 31	❏Dan 7
Dec 26	❏Eccl 8	❏Isa 62	❏2 Chr 32	❏Dan 8
Dec 27	❏Eccl 9	❏Isa 63	❏2 Chr 33	❏Dan 9
Dec 28	❏Eccl 10	❏Isa 64	❏2 Chr 34	❏Dan 10
Dec 29	❏Eccl 11	❏Isa 65	❏2 Chr 35	❏Dan 11
Dec 30	❏Eccl 12	❏Isa 66	❏2 Chr 36	❏Dan 12

Key Events and
Answers to Prayer
That Built Your Hope

_____

_____

_____

_____

_____

_____

_____

_____

_____

_____

_____

_____

_____

_____

_____

_____

_____

_____

_____

_____

_____

_____

Key Events and Answers to Prayer That Built Your Hope

_____

_____

_____

_____

_____

_____

_____

_____

_____

_____

_____

_____

_____

_____

_____

_____

_____

_____

_____

_____

_____

My Journey with God

The primary calling of God on the life of every Christian
is not something you DO. It is something you ARE.
You are being transformed into the likeness of Jesus Christ.

The call to Christ-likeness takes consecration. It takes courage.
It takes integrity, truthfulness, and consistent intimacy with God.
The application of that calling may vary, but the primary calling remains
the same. The Bible says that this calling to Christ-likeness is a
predetermined pattern for everyone who is truly saved. You are predestined
to become like Jesus, if you will yield.

*"For God knew his people in advance, and he
chose them to become like his Son, so that his Son would
be the firstborn, with many brothers and sisters. And
having chosen them, he called them to come to him. And
he gave them right standing with himself, and he
promised them his glory" (Romans 8:29-30).*

Jesus Washing His Disciples' Feet
(logo of Wellington Boone Ministries)

Contact us for resources and more journals in the series
My Journey with God

Wellington Boone Ministries
5875 Peachtree Industrial Blvd.
Suite 300
Norcross, GA 30092

Phone: 770-840-0888

www.apptepublishing.com
www.daretohopejournal.com
www.wellingtonboone.com

Made in the USA
Charleston, SC
02 June 2010